Sustain

Sustain

Extending Improvement in the Modern Enterprise

W. Scott Culberson

BEP BUSINESS EXPERT PRESS

Sustain: Extending Improvement in the Modern Enterprise
Copyright © Business Expert Press, LLC, 2018.

First published in 2018 by
Business Expert Press, LLC
222 East 46th Street, New York, NY 10017
www.businessexpertpress.com

ISBN-13: 978-1-94858-087-8 (paperback)
ISBN-13: 978-1-94858-088-5 (e-book)

Business Expert Press Supply and Operations Management Collection

Collection ISSN: 2156-8189 (print)
Collection ISSN: 2156-8200 (electronic)

Cover and interior design by S4Carlisle Publishing Services Private Ltd., Chennai, India

First edition: 2018

10 9 8 7 6 5 4 3 2 1

Printed in the United States of America.

Dedication

Tu sais.

Abstract

This is a work of system-think on why breakthroughs mostly don't sustain. In answer, it recalls mutual learning, by which the exceptional have defied the norms of decline since before humans could write about it.

Part 1 shows the mechanics how complex adaptive systems extend order—Hayek's *catallaxy*. How lean exploits this is unpacked. Part 2 isolates popular fallacies of control that incentivize undoing. Part 3 offers countermeasures—leveled exploration and exploitation in strategy deployment, standard work, and development of employees, products, services, and methods. Lean turns paradigms and routines from holding on, to sustainably moving on.

Lean is not just a factory thing. Lessons abound in nature's fractals and adaptations, admin, and history too; from the present back through World War II, the Industrial Revolution, the Reformation, to its roots in the civilizing of Antiquity.

Learners mine hard lessons while knowers sadly repeat them. Great sources on *catallaxy*—Juran, Hayek, Popper, Kuhn, Sproul, Rother, March—have left us rich deposits of distilled experience. *Sustain* is a trail guide, locating pivotal insights to defy the entropy of abandon-and-revert, in any enterprise that coordinates resources, time, and treasure in the face of varying, alternative uses.

Keywords

complex adaptive systems, emergence, heterarchy, lean, learning organization, operational excellence, planning, project management, scientific method, standard work, strategic alignment, sustainment

Contents

Foreword

We think our business challenges are new. They are not. Scott shows how mankind and creatures of earth have adapted to challenges like we face over the years. Challenges that at their core are the same, but disguised as new because there are so darned many variables.

He argues, I think successfully for a way of thinking. Understand the past. Focus on the future. Accept the fact that things will change, and today's solutions will be different than yesterday's. If you accept that, you can take the next steps. You can create desire to change because it insures the future. And you can get folks to throw away all the pride that binds you to status quo.

Most importantly, Scott makes it clear the people who are most successful are those who collaborate, learn, and adapt. The great ones are those who bring out the best in people, listen, and try new stuff based on the variables of the day.

This book is like a time machine. Sometimes you feel like you are peering into history. Sometimes you feel like you are staring at your current business and wondering "How'd he know?" Sometimes you will be dreaming of what could be in your future.

As you read this book, you will find uses for old tools, nuggets, and aha moments that could really help you change the culture you manage or work in. Just be prepared to go from ancient times, to academia, to the factory floor and back. Scott will stretch your mind if you let him!

Don Louis
President and CEO
CoLinx, LLC

Using examples found in sports, nature, religion, and history (even early traffic rules), Scott has explained the essence of rules in continuously improving environments, whether they be societal or industrial. This compilation of multiple lifetimes of study and understanding is quite complete as it pertains to the subject of sustainment.

It shows the inevitable overlap of culture with technical problem-solving, highlighting the unintended social consequences of solely technical improvement. He skillfully describes the human nature behind all manner of sustainment rifts and creatively surfaces the importance of mutual learning as the remedy for management hubris.

He describes the pathway toward trust building, leading to mutual ownership and mutual accountability. This is a must-read for everyone who has ever struggled with accelerating or sustaining improvements in an organization, presumably every human being on the planet.

Mike Huszar

President

Drive Incorporated

Acknowledgments

Aaron Styles perceives the themes in torrents of data, clearer than any I know. He wastes no discontent over who his teammates are not: Toward improvement, *he just knows how to go to war with the ones he's got*. He is principled, unruffled, undeterred, neither threatening nor threatened. He has been a true partner in this years-long march to *Sustain*.

Number 8 of Toyota Way's 14 tenets is that things serve us, not us them. Principled tech can turn those words to deeds. I have worked in world-leading operations, in many domains. I find no other who lives Number 8 so adaptably, as Don Louis does at Co-Linx. He does it from a deeply principled view of people. How lucky I am to have his advice and example.

Mike Huszar is a strategic leader in engineering/operations. He is uniquely able to hold those two domains in complement. He brings together what was never meant to be separate and competing to begin with. I am glad to know his insight and distance-vision.

In the word *obtention*, the French unify the disciplines of quality, lean, and innovation. It means *obtaining* value: not just end-control, but value through concept, execution, and sustainment. Bob Miron spent 30 years in obtention of performance, innovation, and marketing of premier tires for Michelin, multi-nationally. This writing benefitted much from his insight on making these propositions accessible. *Merci, mon ami.*

Chris Larson at Ligonier has been a sounding board on historical, civilizational, *deep structures* underlying the ancient principles of improve and sustain. Why $>>$ What $>$ How we will do something. I count myself fortunate to call Chris friend and advisor.

It is the hardest task to explain complexity simply, without becoming simplistic. Dr. Joy Field is a leader in operations management at Boston College. Her perspective was helpful in getting the ideas across.

My wife Anne is the most remarkable person I know, or ever will. In perceiving others rightly, being honest with myself, and gathering so wide a selection of sources into one work, she has been invaluable. Like the author of *Factory Physics* put it: *I thank the One who gave me breath. Each day I draw that breath, I am grateful to share with the woman who takes it away.*

Introduction and Overview

Given the unsustainability of perfect robustness, we need a mechanism by which the system regenerates itself continuously by using, rather than suffering from, random events, unpredictable shocks . . . and volatility.[1]

—Nassim Taleb

Structured application of the lean practices routinely returns the investment several times over, usually in months. It's stunning. Over and again, firms turn back existential threats and post record gains on basics of operational excellence. Case studies are made of the outcomes in safety, quality, delivery, productivity, stakeholder value, and citizenship.

These breakthroughs share one feature that is even more reliably stunning than the confidence of payoff: Count on 90 percent + of the beneficiaries to abandon-and-revert within a couple of years. Many begin well, then allow things to come between them and cashing-in some more.

What This Book Is

This is a study of the exceptions who *sustain*. Failure to do so is the overwhelming norm. This feature seems as irrational as it is universal. It begs explanation, and to be countered.

The literature on improvement centers on how to implement. Most authors warn, and change agents lament, that sustainment is likely to go underserved. The old chorus is a familiar one. We haven't come to retell the sadness of it. We bring to the subject a set of principles and applications that can reset a firm's default from backsliding, to adaptive advance as a norm.

We find answers in the approach of mutual learning, so reliably effective that it already delivered us a Renaissance out of the Dark Ages. Our aim is to turn hearts, minds, and hands to daily out-working of those principles. How to conduct this approach is illustrated in history and animated in the object lessons of nature's complex adaptive systems.

We will see how leverage in this pursuit is being renewed and extended by breakthroughs in the understanding of information, recombinant exploration, and complex adaptive systems. But first we will need to recall and embrace the habits of basic blocking and tackling.

In the spirit of Mike Rother's *Toyota Kata*, it would do great good to restore the behaviors of the scientific method into familiarity and common public use. The very attempt will reform many notions we had too easily just supposed or conceded about how improvement works. The practical implication of good principles is that our behavioral reflexes get recalibrated.

We will see how to counter the norm of learning coming undone, by adopting the paradigm and practice of relentless adaptation and re-extension. It will take us three steps to get from here to there:

First, we examine how improvement forms up in complex adaptive systems:

Part 1: Improvement mostly arises on the workings of *self-organization*.

To improve a thing is to invest order into it. The phenomenon called *emergence* can efficiently auto-arrange our noisy variety of interests and contributions. It generates a species of order that continues to re-extend itself in forward-running loops. This is the thing we are seeing when we experience sustainment.

It is the mechanics "under the hood" of lean. Under conditions that promote the forces and workings of emergence, improvement advances (sustains). Where such arrangements get undone, collaborating groups tribally revert.

Seeing how order assembles exposes the counterforces that run to its undoing:

Part 2: Isolates the beliefs, arrangements, and counterforces that drive backsliding.

Misconceptions of how order arises sow and incentivize its undoing. Collaboration gets reshaped and denatured by our notions of how to achieve "control." Processes and people get reconnected in ways that disfavor the adaptive pursuit of discovery among peers. Our popular, expert-centric ways of trying to maintain order, undo that which could have promoted its re-extension into further gains.

We need to organize a set of behavioral routines—*action repertoires*—to institutionalize the influences that promote sustain-and-extend over a natural tendency to abandon-and-revert:

Part 3: Systematizes our approach to that which promotes the re-extension of gain.

System-think informs the sort of improvement that sustains. On it, we form up action routines, as in-context countermeasures against nature's drivers to attrition.

What This Book Is Not

This is no roll call of symptoms, certainly no tool catalog. Enough of those are already written.

Lean is operating philosophy, not a toolset. It dynamically arranges directionally correct pointers and behaviors on our opportunities and problems. It does this in real-time context on the spot. Lean invents and evolves tools as disposable appliances—mere means to an end. The outcome is mutual extension of cooperative discovery, not the prescriptive use of some promotional method.

On a sampling of lean practices, we will dissect the guts of why, when, and where they function. Being able to unpack how a method works clears up where it applies, if needed, blind spots, and pitfalls. We will see how order inadvertently gets undone through misapplication, vogues, and the cheerleading of "tools" for their own sake.

Abandon-and-Revert Is a Sticky Problem

Those who don't learn from history are condemned to repeat it.

So many current-day OpEx "discoveries" are but reenactments of battles already won before in the quality revolution of the 1980s. Crises of the 1970s had spurred a renewal of mutual learning for improvement. Living standards got lifted to new heights. Then, in many quarters, even basic maintenance of the disciplines that got us there took a back seat to affluence and fresher worries.

That there even was a crisis in the 1970s, was surprising in its own way. World War II had put every back against the wall in the 1940s. Commerce, industry, governance, agriculture, and logistics paid dearly to learn to revitalize. Generational success was achieved in the works of Juran, Deming, Crosby, and others. Productivity won a war then lost the peace: Left unrivalled, broad swaths of first-world enterprise abandoned improvement for fresher concerns.

Toyota rose out of (literal) ashes to surpass Ford, on dogmatic application of Ford's own pre-war principles, and *sanctification* paradigms borrowed from Puritanism by Samuel Smiles and others whom Mr. Toyoda and his circle studiously diagnosed.

The tenets of today's OpEx, the 1980s revolution, and World War II revitalization, are recorded anywhere that Puritans intersected with governance, economy, business, and industry. Improvement since Jonathan Edwards' day has developed mostly in terms of methods efficiency, on the sciences of probability, queuing, information, and recombinance. As Ligonier's Chris Larson notes, those are novel *hows*—very economical new pathways to an ancient *what*. Why $>>$ What $>$ How. The underlying *whats* of sustain have changed remarkably little since the 1500s.

That enterprise needed to reboot in 1940 was because the great exertions of change agents like Eli Whitney and his peers, using lean principles on the challenges of the 1800s, got diverted into the "progress" movements of 1890–1930s. *Scientific Management* especially clouded popular notions of control and order, in a great setback of learning for improvement.

Eli Whitney was only echoing what was already expounded by classical liberals like Adam Ferguson (*History of Civil Society*, 1767), and Adam Smith (*Wealth of Nations*, 1776). They already taught what we call pull, 5S, value-add, and self-ordering emergence, to raise peoples out of ruin. In many instances their achievements got overrun in the violence over control that wracked the 1800s.

Nor were the Puritans and classical liberals the inventors of the lean ideas that Samuel Smiles passed from them to Sakichi Toyoda.[2] They were just unpacking works of the Renaissance and the Reformers, on change and improvement.

The Arsenal of Venice in the 1400s is a manufactory echo of very old ideas on improving. Its ingenuity of standardization and interchangeable parts recurs in broken cycles all the way back to Carthage in Africa's First Punic War and the Qin Dynasty of Asia's third century B.C.

Out of the Dark Ages, Erasmus, Reuchlin, Agricola, and a diversity of others like Ibn Rushd (Averroes) recognized that enterprise had reverted to a state not far from needing to "reinvent the wheel." They did a *post-mortem* on the civilizing prosperity that once flourished in Antiquity.[3] Ancient wisdom was locked up in (scattered) Hebrew, Greek, and Latin classics, which a mere handful of Europeans could even read. They extracted know-how out of dead languages.

Martin Luther codified the modern-day written German language. In so doing, he kicked the door open to transmitting the classics into general public use (mutual learning). Others did likewise in the neighboring cultures. The foundations of improvement could now be mined, refined, and advanced efficiently.

Contrary to popular belief, the Chinese—not Gutenberg—invented movable-type printing. Gutenberg's genius lay in adopting the practices of operational excellence into the domain. To use Mike Rother's expression, he transformed a millennium by *Learning to See.* Separately, the tools and materials of printing were fragile technical novelties that didn't play nicely together. But joined craftily together they made a system—not just printing, but publication. On system-think, Gutenberg streamlined vast amounts of the "Eight Wastes" out of the "value stream." Through iterative trial he optimized ink, paper, and typography. He dialed in the challenges of supply, print setup and operation, and distribution. Now reemerging, civilizational order could be efficiently extended in the continental waves of transformation that have rolled since.[4]

Pointers to Key Figures and Concepts in Sustainment

There is not space here to elaborate all the key figures raised in this book. I hope to interest you enough to pick up the trail. Do Toyota's thing and *go-see* for yourself. We can build a glossary of terms as we go. But this book is not meant so much to fill in all the background, as to point it out. We will show where key players and concepts relate into the theme of sustaining. If this book does enough to convince you to go pick up the trail of the great sources it points at, you will discover far better writers than this engineer. *Sustain* is a guidepost.

For an example of what lies behind lean for you, consider Georgius Agricola mentioned above. Most have never heard of this principal force in the recovery of the classics. Admittedly, what got recovered is moral philosophy. Who has the time for it?

Agricola recognized how much it matters for the normals. While Italy's Renaissance ran after the aesthetic arts, Germany bent to the perfection of the industrial, social, and medical arts. Of many reasons, one of the greatest single factors in it breaking this way, was Agricola.

His conviction that ideas have consequences made him a primary force in rolling out general education. Until then, agricultural, industrial, medical, and economic know-hows were the closely held, secret province of experts, passed on through direct apprenticeship. Know-how was kept in human vessels, a narrow elite but the secretive, intellectual, captive property of rulers and magnates. The public welfare bottlenecked at this captive scarcity.

We will hear a lot about *mutuality* in this book. Agricola established it, to break through to a broad range of proprietary lords of know-how. He enlightened how they could codify what was between their ears (zealously guarded). He demonstrated how order could thereby get extended, broadened, and deepened to the mutual prosperity of all concerned.

This was sociological breakthrough. His most known work was *De Re Metallica* (1556), the founding reference of modern geology, mining, and metallurgy. But his other texts were wide-ranging, and prodigious. Unless you are a metallurgist (or a *metalhead*) chances are you never heard of the guy. But elementary education, mining, geology, metallurgy, inorganic chemistry, occupational medicine, safety, health, and hygiene come down to us through his "coaching tree." How he blazed such trails is instructive as we wonder how to sustain now.

Cycles of improvement and backsliding trace all the way back. *History may not repeat, but often it rhymes.* At intervals, this book will take asides from its business and industrial examples, to reinforce with illustrations out of nature and history.

Improvement Is Not Just a Factory Thing

Lean works by forming the kind of connections that promote mutual self-order toward True North. It exploits what F.A. Hayek termed universal *deep structures* in nature's working. These provide us a clever way to harness routine operations, to opportunistically generate forward propulsion, appearing to defy the Second Law.

Termites, badgers, and bluegills exploit this. Markets do it. Our production systems can do it, too. In simple, deterministic systems the gain runs linearly. But in complex adaptive systems, we will see how it explodes exponentially toward the "basins of attraction." This is powerful stuff.

Nature (human, otherwise) holds universal tendencies that counter such arrangements. Lean offers answering principles to **sustain any endeavor that coordinates materials, human resources, time, and treasure in face of variable, alternative uses.**

"Lean" practices were ordering and extending civilization—nature, language, manufacture, trade, agriculture, exploration—before humans could read or write. Lean precedes and far exceeds shallow stereotypes of Ford, things Japanese, or Toyota (remarkable as it is). Don't settle for cartoonish, mystical notions of lean as *sensei* gimmicks for factories.

Instead, do system-think. Of course we will explore factory examples. Intentionally we will draw a greater number of parallels from admin, nature, and history. Consider how the *deep structures* of improvement, which are universal, can translate into your own situation.

Ad Fontes

Against the decline of the Dark Ages, Erasmus' advice was *ad fontes—to the sources.*[5] I took it.

Those who aspire to being learners (learning organization) owe a special debt to Joseph Juran, F.A. Hayek, Thomas Kuhn, Karl Popper, James March, Roger Schwarz, Mike Rother, and R.C. Sproul. They ranged far and wide from one another. Each has contributed distinctive, but complementary, insights into the challenges to sustaining.

Paradigms are the ability to spot resemblances between seemingly disparate problems. Every reviewer of this text remarked how often going to a new paragraph shot them from one domain to another, entirely different, or into another era. It is intentional. Showing it this way bears out a key paradigm: Breakthrough is a universal sequence. Letting it lapse is a universal failure mode.

Because we labor in disparate areas, the commonalities of sustainment are not always visible on the surface. Most of the references on improvement tilt to manufacturing, agriculture, and medicine. Service, admin, design, and the creative arts have not seen that level of treatment.

We need to jailbreak the paradigms of sustainment out of the mental confines of barnyards and factory ghettoes. Physics is physics. People are people. Tenets of sustainment are timeless. *Sustain* is going to throw daylight across disparate parallels of domains and eras. We can learn from the lapses of most others. But we will really learn from that diverse minority who worked out sustainment.

Dovetailing such an eclectic mix into one readable flow has been a tall order. When it bogged down, I just kept coming back to finding that there could hardly be a more pressing topic for the doers I meet, across this nation.

Where this writing comes up short on style, consider its chapters as trail markers, pointing back at the great sources on learning enterprise. You deserve my best and I have given it.

Now, here we go—*Ad Fontes*

PART 1

The Mechanics
of Self-Organizing Systems

Part 1: Improvement mostly arises on the workings of self-organization.

The phenomenon called *emergence* can efficiently auto-arrange our noisy variety of interests and contributions, to generate a species of order that continues to re-extend itself in forward-running loops. This is the thing we are seeing when we experience sustainment.

It is the mechanics "under the hood" of Lean. Under conditions that promote the forces and workings of emergence, improvement advances (sustains). Where such arrangements get undone, collaborating groups tribally revert.

CHAPTER 1

Rule-Connected

The possibility of extending an order of peace, beyond the small group which could agree on particular ends . . . is due to the discovery of a method of collaboration which requires agreement only on means and not on ends.[1]

—F.A. Hayek

The Core Principle of Group Improvement

Tribal society is end-connected. Extended orders are rule-connected.

Effective Interests Are Personal

It is simplistic to think of the public interest like a sort of benevolent harmonic that the good guys can somehow feel and resonate to. A society is not a sentient being: It has no singular interest per se. The same goes for departments, which are comprised of persons.

That everyone possesses interests of their own seems undeniable. Any motivational scheme that discounts this is magical thinking.

Fortunately, recognizing that every person is a self does not require that we surrender to coercive selfishness to work out the arrangement of scarce resources among us. As we will see, the simple genius of self-arranging order gives us a better way.

Even the gentlest of individual interests collide, even within one's own heart. Resource limits force each of us to curtail our ambitions. Then all must be bent still further to work out a coexistence with the pursuits of those around us. When trying to reconcile it all in the heat of compromise, abstractions on behalf of some nameless, faceless "public good" can't suffice to show us what to do on the spot.

We get somewhere when we recognize that an enterprise is a mutuality of individuals—the ones we see plus unknowable others we can't—affecting and affected down long webs of supply and distribution. Public interest is best seen as what would serve the greatest **number** and **extent** of the vast swirl of individual interests, whether known to us personally or not.

We Could Do Primitive

Given land and seed, a hermit does not have to be concerned with others' rules. Hermits settle differences over allocation of scarce things via conflict: win-lose.

But solitary effort is primitive. It can't yield the calories or variety either side would gain (and contribute) were this hermit to become a member of a group practicing specialization.

We Could Do Tribal

It expands the welfare of both tribe and hermit beyond the sum of their separate harvests, if they join to extend specialization. They join their separate means in subscription to rules that enshrine what is each one's fair share of contributing and payoff. Submission to a shared aim, a common *end*, is what connects tribe members.

Within a group, the form of shared aim we signed on to is what we now use to settle resource issues peaceably. Conflict is still what is used to settle differences beyond tribe (those "others" who don't subscribe to our aims and ends).

Tribal arrangements are not abstract—they are concrete and quite tangible. Members can see the collective stockpile, know the others, and are known. Uniformity of ends is thus visible and enforced. Keeping the peace depends on it. A standalone group is **end-connected**.

We Extend Order by Becoming Abstract Rule-Connected

As we go along, some other group may show comparative advantage in some of the things we do. Breaking isolation to rely on another's services where it makes sense can mutually extend both groups to higher outcomes. If not, the parties walk away and keep doing their own thing. We can categorize this as the benefit of *specialization*.

Notice the seen and the unseen: When as suppliers we deliver a portion of our stuff over to others to add the next step of value to it, we no longer control and see it here. What we *can* now see is a lessened stockpile here, in the name of something abstract "others" do, out there somewhere.

To up-order usually involves linking up into some new interparty system that collaboratively rearranges the resources and the work. This increases the number, complexity, and abstraction of relationships comprised in the system.

Mutual Extension Generates Higher Orders: Abstract, in Levels

In your hands, you hold an example. I composed this work on a MacBook Pro computer. It consists of dozens of subsystems, connected in highly specific ways. Each subsystem has tens of components, connected in specific ways. Each component consists of raw materials joined in specific ways. Delete or recombine at any of those levels, and this pile of parts ceases to act like—to be—that productivity-multiplying appliance called a Mac.

At a tangible level, base materials for the display possess properties like opacity. At +1 level abstraction, a screen gains properties like transparency. Its materials didn't have that. Assembly endows a hard drive with +1 level abstract ability to store code. Parts can't do that. At +1 above subsystems is an assembled, cold Mac. Invisible electricity gives that system +1 energetic potential. Configured software adds +1 functionalities, real but not physical.

On the phenomenon of *emergence,* favorable arrangements join parts into a system of more abstract capabilities than its subunits. *How we connect within and between layers is what extends systems to new levels of use and order.* This turns out to be the crux of sustaining.

My Mac could have set on my desk until the end of time, and *Sustain* would not have written itself. I used it as means to connect my experiences and education, with many others' (some living, many long gone), to form these extended levels of thought on sustainment.

Apple delivered a Mac on abstract credit on my card account. They had no idea if I would play games, write a book, compose hip hop, or toss it in the Indian Ocean. They furnished a platform that makes it incredibly efficient to extend collaboration, to degrees I would not have believed 15 years ago. I took them up on it.

Apple advanced the cause of sustainment, not by attempting to prescribe specific time-and-place activity they knew in advance and endorsed. It was left to me to explore what novel outcomes a Mac could help me creatively gin up, out of the kinds of connections it could open.

Now you can go reconnect the ideas of this book, to boost sustainment in domains that have never yet crossed my mind.

Civilization

Wherever we form up an extended order, now it becomes agreements, not conflicts, which allocate scarce resources among the actors. This is the principle of *civilization*: It expands the list of "others" with whom agreement must hold. Extension makes it impossible to know all the others, their aims, and ends "over there." They can't know all of us either. Risk and reward get decoupled, in complex systems. A wide web of participants become **abstract rule-connected.**

This creates faith challenges: seen versus unseen. Can I reliably expect to receive better, later, in return for what I sent? Why shouldn't I break the law, where it is certain I won't be caught?

As ventures scale up complexity, the span of affected persons and resources widens. Accounting (what do we have, who has claim to it?) becomes quite **abstract.**

Commands versus Rules: Understanding the Difference

Resources may be used in many, alternative ways. To allocate them is to manage. We can do so by commands or by rules. We should be clear about the difference in terms:

Commands

Commands prescribe **ends**—action and allocation of specific resources, actors, times and places, toward specific outcomes. Commands direct the *matter* to be done.

Computing analogy: **Think of commands as executable instructions**.

Some is necessary, but the directing of ends is a net resource taker (-). End-connection uses an executor: It burdens a system. The less we must do, the more efficient.

Rules

Or we may manage through **abstract² rules**. Rules do not prescribe specific allocation of actor, resource, time, place, or personal ends. They apply to an unknowable number of potential future instances. In other words, rules prescribe *behavior*, the *manner* of doing.

Rules say how to stay in bounds of mutual connection, while prosecuting our several aims. Rules circumscribe *how*. *What* to do in the moment is mostly left up to the actors. As it turns out, motivated people use good imagination.

Computing analogy: **Think of rules as the operating system**.

Wherever rules form up based on the mutuality of the manner how the actors are willing to connect, rules turn out to be net-producers (+), not resource consumers. Here, gain adaptively self-arranges in novel extensions of what Hayek termed *spontaneous order*. Complexity up-fits itself without the expense and lag of an orchestra conductor.

This form of management delivers unmatched efficiency, by entrusting the ends to what Hayek called a *discovery process* among the peers. Leadership focuses on providing, promoting, and protecting the adaptive rearrangement of *means* by those on the spot.

In complexity, we are more discoverers than knowers. We entrust the conversion of means into outcomes, to the ones on the spot. For as far as they are clever enough to extend it. So long as they operate in bounds of the rules. Leaders mostly have to just keep shoveling coal to *The Little Engine That Could*. Be sure to file this away for later talk on *hoshin kanri* (strategic alignment).

A Doctor's Office Analogy

Context	Appointments must be preapproved, 1 week in advance.
Today's command	Doctor will see Elise at 9:00 a.m. Bob at 9:20. Dan at 9:40 . . .
	We'll see the rest of you at your appointments (next week or later).
?	*What if X is delayed and misses a slot? It goes unused.*
?	What *if an injured child won't live until an appointment?*
Rule-based	We can think up rule-based systems that serve much better than the command system above. For instance, an appointment grid with slots left for walk-ins. Hayek observed on this scenario:

Mothers who could never agree whose desperately ill child the doctor should attend first will readily agree before the event that it would be in the interest of all if he attended the children on some regular order which increased his efficiency.[3]

To extend order (thus complexity), we must concede the *impossibility* of ends-management that insists we know the others, approve their uses of "our stuff," and hold to shared aims and ends. That is just plain not doable in complex enterprise.

What *is* doable is an *abstract* rule-set that prescribes mutually agreed behaviors, not personal outcomes.[4] Even rivalry, so long as it is rule-following, extends welfare further than we could as hermits or tribes striving unconstrained by submission to mutual rules.

Spontaneous order, were it the product of expert planners, would be celebrated among the signal achievements of humanity.

The discovery that by substituting abstract rules of conduct for obligatory concrete ends . . . enabled each individual to gain from the skill and knowledge of others whom he need not even know and whose aims could be wholly different from his own.[5]

An abstract rule-set aggregates mutual learning, to fuel self-organization in a system.

> Most of the knowledge on which we rely in the pursuit of our ends is the unintended by-product of others exploring the world in different directions from those we pursue ourselves, because they are impelled by different aims.[6]

Order is extended, not by enforcement of one common aim, but through commitment to an abstract rule-set to serve, guide, and bind all the actors equally in their pursuit of their aims.

> Members benefit from each other's efforts not only in spite of, but often even because of, their several aims being different.[7]

The Fallacy of Single, Collective Purpose

Commands prescribe specific action, on time, on the spot (as Toyota might call it, *in the gemba*). This type of order cannot reach very far.

Rules serve a broader purpose. Where we leave discovery a space to hunt, agents run in creative pursuit of gain, within bounds of mutual rules. They arrange novel up-ordering of their collaboration. Frequently this draws in new collaborators, to extend the gain. Hayek termed emergent, cooperative rearrangement like this *extended order*.

> [Rules] serve not to make any particular plan of action successful, but to reconcile many different plans of action.[8]

When crises threaten, leaders sound the call for all to keep resolve. From there it is only a small step to demanding singleness of purpose. On the surface, distinction between the two sounds like knit-picking semantics. But this thinking embeds a fallacy in how we view others.

Especially now, these interdependents need to be as good as they can be at coordinating their several interests. We cannot afford for them to divert scarce energy on presumption that bosses can cheerlead the inconvenience out of nature or legislate the personal interests out of the subordinates.

We adapt more and more, not to the particular circumstances, but so as to increase our adaptability to kinds of circumstances which may occur. The horizon of our sight consists mostly of means, not of particular ultimate ends.[9]

Groups get worn down by poor handling of their differences. Visions of HR utopia, single-minded co-labor, sound lovely. But this Trojan Horse mindset holds unintended consequences. To insist on subscription to common purpose as integral to collaboration is to see others who hold differing aims as obstacles, enemies essentially. Ideas have consequences.

The fallacy of common aims is a condescension that other-izes those who diverge from my interests. It dresses up to look upbeat and unifying, but it sows fundamental division. It is an atavistic reflex—a reversion to tribal impulse. In times of crisis, group-think (well-meaning or not) drives order, discovery, civility, and enterprise straight into recession.

What really aids all concerned in the time of need is not external conformity but real diversity, humility, and tolerance within the bounds of the rules.

No Claim That Extended Order Is Panacea

Individuals and groups suffer setbacks through no fault of their own. No system is perfect in wisdom and foresight. No one can claim that an extended order will make everything rosy for every party, every time.

Looking back over history, we can say confidently though that figuring out an extended order serves the greatest span of interests and extent of any arrangement ever devised. Abstract rule-connection is adaptive. Even out of setbacks and crises collaborators can rise in pursuit of their interests to form up behaviors of protection and recovery. An extended order leverages mistakes and misfortunes into a *discovery process* on behalf of the afflicted.

Exploiting Dispersed Knowledge

The public wins when a maximum of individuals subscribe to a simple rule-set that applies evenly to all. Each one's pursuits within rules serve to **link up their fractional, dispersed knowledge.** Hayek's word for this, the apex form of adaptation, was *catallaxy.*[10]

Its rule-sets adapt not to the noise of personal, *particular* circumstances. Rather, things run to an imperative that the group relentlessly increases its adaptability to *kinds* of circumstances.[11]

Catallaxy is characterized by use of brilliant, simple, symbolic guidance like price or Takt, to signal and coordinate the actors on mutual, strategic basins of attraction. The act itself of a routine task contributes my local, partial knowledge in the moment, on the spot. In one stroke, it pulls all the others' current information sum to me and updates theirs. Each can exploit this extension of knowledge to achieve better than they might individually, tribally, or as lagged and filtered by a central planner. This is how nature, and lean practices, can do like they do.

> there will exist no agreement on the relative importance of their respective ends. There would exist . . . open conflict of interests if agreement were necessary as to which particular interests should be given preference over others.[12]

The meek and the proud, hungry, overfed, materialistic, sacrificially unselfish, spiritual and profane, who never will know one another, will never agree on "ideal" aim. But all can agree on what constitutes an agreeable *way* to coordinate toward their several ends.

We reap the benefits of *catallaxy* every day in replenishment pull, traffic circles, pricing, skating rinks, language formation, internet routing, 5S and so on.

> Individuals are not required to agree on ends but only on means which are capable of serving a great variety of purposes and which each hopes will assist him in his own purposes.[13]

To the Sources

An aim of this book is to point up the great sources, so that readers might go, underscore, and mine the details on key veins. There are already two sources we should note:

> *Use of Knowledge in Society*[14] is a good primer on extended order— brief and profound.

Self-Organization in Biological Systems[15] is an explanatory survey of object lessons on emergence and sustainment in the complex adaptive systems of nature. On the same mechanics as markets, and lean practices like 5S and pull, even the lowliest of unsupervised animals exploit a tiny handful of rules into stunning exhibits— beehives, anthills, lightning bug synchronization, nesting fractals, hunting symbiosis, fish schooling.[16] Even nonliving crystals and chemicals extend order in breathtaking displays. Parallels for business and industrial behavior are instructive. Be forewarned— you will marvel.

Action Repertoires as Discovery Processes[17]

Military parallels are useful. Patrols go out to check zones, not to attend scheduled skirmish dates with opponents. The age-old practice that Toyota calls *go-see* positions them to discover information needed to advance (avoid ruinous surprise). A key feature of sustainment is the behavior of iteratively patrolling to a rule-set: Patrols walk out not so much a script, as an adaptive template that promotes discovery under kinds of situations likely to come up.

Under dynamic circumstances, to pre-script the chess moves and outcomes would be to expect participants to pass up any advantage of combined knowledge they might gain on the spot. It would ask them to subordinate plain interests to an inflexible edict that may now be not even as good as the fragmentary way a hermit could have approached things.

General welfare is diminished, wherever the scheme expects others to forego mutuality of knowledge, when instead they could collaboratively extend on the spot. The cognitive planning-centric form of organization asks the actors to settle for centralized, scripted direction predicated on information that is fragmentary, dated, or worse.

Greatest welfare emerges when the widest number pursue the broadest array of interests, to the fullest extent their joined knowledge can inform. The effective *discovery process* is bounded by abstract rules of behavior, not some strong leader's naive insistence on undeviating, shared aims.

Thermodynamic

Living systems are thermodynamic,[18] which is to say, converters of materials captured from surroundings, into their fuel. So long as the system is supplied with energy it advances toward a higher state, complexity. Cut off the energy, and the Second Law reminds us that things left to themselves decay toward disorder, or deconstruction (in a "closed system").

Our bodies are a marvel in that when food is cut off we don't instantly decompose. We self-order in what runs counter to the dreaded entropy. Hunger and stress impel us to creative feats. What fuels this is a clever storage system.

When times are good we preserve some of the captured energy as fat. Deposits of potential energy are dispersed across the system. These deposits power adaptation and advancement and flexibly fuel the way through the uncertainties of future circumstance.

The provision of access to these depots enables our system to behave as an "open system". Here it gets really interesting. Hungry bodies draw from unseen deposits to arrange and advance in a way that looks like it is flaunting the Second Law. Fat is quite the device. Yet there is another, even more impressive: Rules are the ultimate, densest crystallization of potential energy—stored information.

Through positive and negative feedback, those who will go to *gemba* become informed as to the potentialities of all manner of materials, behaviors, and circumstances. With determination, accumulated learning sifts into patterns. It dawns on the observant that certain arrangements tend to create favorable conditions for self-assembly and attraction toward a higher order, not decay.

Mutual self-interest (not selfishness) *sets the directionality of system attractors.* Rules emerge as the distillate of experience: They are the accumulated wisdom about kinds of arrangements to favor formation of gain. The rule-set informs collaborators toward structural stability.

Mostly Prohibition, Not Much Prescription[19]

Paraphrasing John Locke, it is *operating conduct*, not outcomes, that rules oversee.[20]

A rule-set gets worked out in advance of difficult, scarce resource allocations. This reassures all that none gained privilege at the expense of colleagues, in the run-up to a contentious tradeoff. Prequalified mutuality means low drag. Reassurance begets flexibility—actors can confidently press situational advantage wherever the act of extending collaboration reveals it in the moment.

Amendment of rules should be transparent. Amendment is stabilized over a duration long enough to keep confidence that the rules won't get bent in the middle of the game, in ways that privilege some at the others' expense.

Abstract rules demystify cooperation. Mainly they set boundaries of action not available to the subscribers. This defuses conflict and withdrawal, by reducing uncertainty among potential rivals. The rules delineate behaviors all can count on—what property and services are open for use. They enable us to reliably predict the behavior of others (most of whom are unknown to us).

Non-instinctive

> To early thinkers the existence of an order of human activities transcending the vision of an ordering mind seemed impossible. Even Aristotle . . . still believed that order . . . could extend only so far as the voice of a herald could reach.[21]

Useful as it is, the rule-set does suffer the hardship of being abstract, not instinctual. It must be bought into, to hold. Another great source, Hayek's *The Fatal Conceit*, does a nice job of unpacking our love–hate relationship with abstract rules:

> They not only could hear their herald; they usually knew him personally. . . . It was mainly . . . shared aims and perceptions that coordinated. . . . Coordination depended decisively on instincts of solidarity . . . applying to members of one's own group, but not to others.[22]

Ancestors who collaborated ran circles around *nature red in tooth and claw*, on simple practices of safe passage, property rights, truthfulness, contract, fair measure, competition, and the like.

an isolated man would soon have been a dead man. The primitive individualism described by Thomas Hobbes is hence a myth. The savage is not solitary. . . . There was never a war of all against all.[23]

Primal instinct does not contain these distillations of stored knowledge. Rules are discoveries from trial, learnings that have to be passed on by encoding, teaching, and mentor modeling.

Mankind achieved civilization by developing and learning to follow rules . . . that often forbade him to do what his instincts demanded, and no longer depended on a common perception of events.[24]

Instead of tribal fight or flight, we could now transcend situations where only some have fragments of the knowledge needed to form up a good allocation. We could now stretch order far beyond the narrow range of solutions where all affected persons know what there is to know and are unanimous (or compelled into submission) as to what to do next.

Constraints on the instinctual practices of human nature are reflexively hated.

Myths of Authority in How Rule-Sets Come to Be

It is natural to assume that because certain time-honored rules produced great results, they must have come down from a planned stroke of design + authority. Fables invent heroes like this. But history tells it another way. This was a great civilizational rediscovery of the Reformation and Counter-Reformation.

Citizens whose interests suffer uncertainty in the absence of *rule of law* do not (willingly) cede unthinking say-so to appointed masterminds and rule-makers. Hated, ineffective, stagnant rules eventually get thrown over. Great rules endure ultimately not on authority, but because they contain effectiveness and mutuality.

It would be naive to imagine that all achievements and rules came down out of kind justice. Even rogues have sustained notably. Great rules last not because of saintliness of angelic lawgivers, but bottom-line because they promote effectiveness through mutuality.

Those whose reputations now attach to the great rules in some way found arrangements that worked, to a degree of mutuality. Were this not so, it would not stick. The revered experts had the insight to adapt the way to their formulations. Their tries progressively extended the interests of the affected enough to awaken mutual interest in upholding the rule.

> Theirs was an authority derived from their . . . capacity to **find** justice, not to create it.[25]

Atavism[26]

Human beings are powerfully wired to gratify impulsive reflex. Restraint is learned behavior. History is a long tale of groups refining methods of coercion as their answer to scarcity and uncertainty. Then along have come great exceptions, where rivals (re)discovered a more prosperous (peaceful) coexistence made possible through arranged extensions of mutuality.

Catallaxy is tolerance—a form of acceptance confident and mature enough that it has to neither yield nor demand acquiescence. The rule-set is inclusive in this sense. But it is also exclusive, in that it prohibits the sort of insecurity that equates progress to submitting the neighbors to my prescribed aims. Its beneficiaries need only bind themselves by a simple, abstract, mutually favorable rule-set equal for all. This is arguably the greatest discovery ever made.

The first time we notice a self-ordering process like the lean practice of *kaizen*, we tend to interpret the order produced as if a mastermind must have cognitively designed its steps and its ends. This endows leaders with too much credit and blame. It is simplistic to suppose that the primary cause of outcomes is the agency of leaders. Such is hero worship. Mutuality falls into despotism when leaders start believing too much of the hype about their great judgment. This runs to diminished diversity of interests allowed (choking off what fuels discovery). This runs to recession, then insubordination (an especially destructive way to evolve fallible rules).

> [One following these rules] even though he depends on them for life, does not and usually cannot understand how they function or how they benefit him.[27]

Learning to See Rules Scientifically

Lean is very efficient at finding beneficial behavioral value propositions. It captures learning in the form of abstract rules. These standards codify the most order-extending arrangement of behavior (thus resources) known to be available in a circumstance. *Takt* attainment, *hansei*, replenishment, and Standard Work toggles are lean examples of such value propositions.

A value proposition is a "prediction". To the scientific method we go, to test it:

> We use **P**lan, **D**o, **C**heck, and **A**djust (PDCA) to inform periodic deep reflection, from which we standardize. Then we restart our foraging from the newly informed vantage point.

We leave off superstition, and get into real science, when we stop seeing standards as capital-T Truth claims: They are, instead, behavioral value propositions that demand constant testing and reiteration to hold. This opens the door to sometimes reformation.

Why >> What > How

When we are being weighed in the balances of scarcity, sticking by a rule-set on principle, just feels counterintuitive.

Examples of Lean Precepts That Feel Countercultural

Fallacy of push	Fallacy of batching	*Jidoka*—stop to fix issues
Fallacy of "multitasking"	Fallacy of overproduction	Fallacy of point efficiency
Go slow so you can go fast	"Right-the-first-time" fallacy	Fallacy of the "trivial" many

Rule-connection bucks tribal, fight-or-flight reflex. As order extends, its value propositions are real, but they become increasingly abstract.

Drivers of This Counter-intuitiveness of Abstract Rules

- Some folks are just more literal than abstract.
- Perseverance is hard. Old hands waver in belief in the unseen or delayed gratification.

- Workforces turn over. Newcomers don't see the unseen scope of interests that led others to form rules. They naturally have less enthusiasm to guard and extend others' arrangements.
- Novices can't apply or improve rules not rightly trained, explained, retained to them.
- New leaders undermine stored knowledge out of *hubris* or ignorance.
- Position and reward accrue to who holds the rule book. Specialists have incentive to resist new improvement if it means new arrangements. Specialization morphs into *hierarchy*.
- Things change. Even if there had ever been a perfect rule-set, it would need to evolve.
- To extend order takes effort and risk. In times of plenty, future want is theory. Enjoying today's windfall requires neither effort nor imagination, so there is inertia.
- Learners continually discover ways that could extend the welfare to new reaches. At first it is unclear if/how the old rule-set can be made to serve.

These forces tend to the neglect, decay, and bypassing of rules rather than the harder slog of improving them. Among bosses this runs to frozen stasis, and a compliance-cop view on the status quo. This perverts the intended notion of standards, scientifically speaking.

Where these counterforces take hold, they make a permanent underclass of workers who abandon hope of mutuality in any sense of improving to their own aims. Learning and coaching are needed to continually reenergize against the entropy of selfishness or atavism, which creep so naturally into the relationships of workers and leaders.

Lecture and edict won't do. Learned advantage behaviors (abstract) must be modeled to be grasped. Underlying propositions should remain something that gets refreshed by the affected. One way to help this is effective onboarding. That means not just to convey how to do external rituals of conformity on the rule-set. Right training also renews the underlying intent out of which those acts were designed. This leverages onboarding into an occasion to continually refresh. It makes a feedback loop, not a one-way conveyance of some unchanging capital-T Truth claim.

Maintaining *consent of the governed* is a never-ending challenge of leadership.

Seeing how order forms, points up how it degrades. This is important, but it is still philosophy. Saying w*hy* hasn't (yet) laid out *how* to form a rule-set for emergence at your place. Abstractions won't move orders on a customer's demand.

In this first chapter, we saw what a rule-set is and what it does. Now is there something we can go do about that?

- In Chapter 2 we will see how to build an actual rule-set, from scratch, taking the example of an intersection.
- In Chapter 3 we will then survey a host of lean techniques, from 5S to *kanban* and beyond. We will examine how the rule-set functions. This will help relate the broad applicability of the principle of extended order to other domains.

CHAPTER 2

Forming an Effective Rule-Set

Structures to facilitate discovery, communication, storage of knowledge.[1]

—Steve Fleetwood

A means to prevent clashes between conflicting aims and not a set of fixed ends.[2]

—F.A. Hayek

In American football, a rule-set is the set of keys and reads players are trained to make, to choose best action on the spot. A coach isn't in the line of scrimmage to micromanage the instantaneous multitude of choices at 11 positions. Once the ball is snapped, momentary choices belong to players. Coaches train them into the capacity to execute and put them in position to do so.

The coach synthesizes a great number of observations on potential challenges. He catalogs attacks, strengths, weaknesses, and tendencies. He organizes a set of mental models that strip away "eye candy." He distills situational recognition down to a handful of symbolic cues, which he drills players to recognize.

To these he associates behavioral reflexes that counter opponents' intent, and flip circumstances to advantage his team's aims. Through a regimen of practice, film study, and mental reps, team and coach drill to the point of reflexive recognition and response.

Kata

In 2010, Mike Rother led the scientific method in a jailbreak from "credentialing." He breached walls of authority, status, and "belts" to bring improvement back into the imagination of the working public. He achieved escape velocity—intuitive grasp across sociological lines. He captured the behavioral essence of real science in an unbreakably simple idea—the martial arts paradigm of *action repertoires*.

> In Japan such patterns or routines are called **kata** (noun).[3]

> If an organization wants to thrive by continually improving and evolving, then it needs systematic procedures and routines—methods—that channel our human capabilities and achieve the potential.[4]

> Think Karate Kid: *wax on, wax off, wax on, wax off.* To effectively promote spontaneous order, rules will be few, simple, concise, reducible to visual and reflexive cues, of general applicability. We unpacked this in the prior chapter.

> Members can face unpredictable and uncertain situations . . . with confidence and effective action, because they have learned a behavioral routine . . . a competitive advantage.[5]

Applications

Moses

The world's most famous judge spent 40 years elaborating right and wrong in countless specific cases. Yet the Commandments, out of which he drew all those detailed applications of time and place, were a mere 10 in number.

Hammurabi

The world's oldest written legal code, the *Code of Hammurabi*, is inscribed on a stone that could fit on a coffee table. It was sufficient to encompass the rule of Babylon.

> Agents, acting purposefully or consciously, unconsciously draw upon, and thereby reproduce, the structures that govern their actions in daily life.[6]

Termites

On a handful of elementary rules simple, unsupervised termites build mounds that are nature's most complex non-excavated structures, spanning meters high and wide, with adaptive supply, defense, and even temperature regulation to a couple of degrees.[7]

Bees

Simple rule-guided worker bees flex unsupervised to construct, feed, maintain, defend, heat, cool, and extend their colonies. They are ceaseless and resilient against waves of continuously varying challenge, opportunity, resource-richness, and availability.[8]

The above are natural and administrative analogs for how to be effective in complex enterprise. Which of a wide allowable range of actions to choose depends on the spot details. Even if some great wizard of planning could know how to prescribe the minutiae of wise action in advance, the attempt to do so would regulate to the point of smothering the actors and the opportunity.

Airplanes

In *Product Development Flow* Donald Reinertsen illustrates the rule-set idea in how weight and cost were reconciled, with better flow in design of the Boeing 777.

Initial target total weight and cost were divvied out to the subsystems, as a performance envelope that each must meet. Allocating upfront in so complex a system was speculative. Globally, it makes sense to allow a subsystem to transgress its weight or cost limit, if it causes neighbors to pay it back in multiples of their own reductions made possible. Unfortunately, a subsystem's own allowance gives a local team no obvious view on system-level opportunities like this. Suboptimization is inevitable.

Where a 777 subsystem was allocated a liberal share of total cost but a meager weight share, it promoted overly expensive design tradeoffs for meager weight gains. Reinertsen's example has such a team pursuing weight reduction at increased design cost of $5,000 per pound. If a neighboring system got allocated a tight share of cost, but generous weight, its incentive was to pass up even cheap design ideas that could shed weight. The example has such a team passing up weight savings that cost only $50 per pound.

To counter they might (theoretically) funnel designs to a central arbiter, to take on weight through a global tradeoff effort. This supposes that the referee could know and be available enough to perceive and trade off subsystems' details in terms of impact overall, on an objectively fair basis. Even if feasible this would be ineffectively slow.

> Instead, Boeing calculated a decision rule . . . at the **system** level. Any designer was authorized to increase unit cost by up to $300, by making design changes or material substitutions, to save a pound of weight. As a result, Boeing had 5,000 engineers making system-level optimum trade-offs without the need to ask permission.

> the superiors didn't actually give up control over the decision. Instead, they recognized that they could still control the decision without participating in it. They simply had to control the economic logic of the decision.[9]

Emergence is nimble because simple rules can do all of the following, in the instant:

- On reflex, with no need of out-of-cycle analysis, arbiters, or third-party experts it displays what range of allowable action is open to them;
- It arranges, coordinates, points the actors on best next step;

- ○ On a heading that best pursues their several aims, without compromising mutuality with the other stakeholders,
- ○ toward the global attractor, not just personal, local optimization.

Detailed choice of action is entrusted to the ones on the spot. They are better-informed than any coach could be over by the bench. The interactors allocate scarce resources simply by acting upon the signals in the circumstance, on the heading pointed by the rules.

In Chapter 3, we will survey the mechanics of how some common OpEx methods employ a rule-set to guide reflexive coordination, to tremendous efficiency and effect.

Illustrating the Rule-Set: An Intersection

Vehicles have lifted great burdens of labor. At first, price was high, owners few, and speeds low. Intersecting was rare so drivers just got by, by making it up on the spot. But when it did happen those individuals did have to figure something out.

Demand rose, price fell, usage extended into new opportunities, and ownership grew. The aims of more and more were fulfilled, until trails evolved into roads, into systems. Traffic and conflicts of aim multiplied, leading to conflict, injury, and damage.

A simple crossing is a shared resource. Avoiding collision means only one can occupy it at a time. When more than one desires use in the same moment, it must get allocated—one way or another. Some ways are more satisfying to more aims/extent than are others.

Direct Meeting

Early on, "figuring out" would mean stating and reconciling aims. That can hardly be done while moving, at a distance, over noise. Intersecting would have been tantamount to a meeting invitation—a frustration of all drivers' aims. They would welcome a way to keep rolling.

Hand Signals

Gestures can signal intent of turns that don't involve crossing. But they offer nothing to allocate priority among crossers. Games of chicken won't relieve the loss (sum of waiting by all parties, injury, damage). Bluff and force would only make things worse. Anyone not convinced on principle should take a lap around the *Arc de Triomphe*.

We could guess at the intentions of others, and preset our own courses based on assumption. All drivers would need to guess correctly—fast— for this to work. Probability is low. Price of assuming wrong is high, and cost to society remains high.

The Traffic Cop

We could station wardens at every intersection to query the arriving drivers, or assume. Or they could ration on a basis of time in line, or bribes. In any case, cops would observe-orient-decide-transmit. Drivers would inform-wait-receive-orient-act.

Summed over all the drivers, waiting loss is high. Ability to process all the aims degrades exponentially with number of drivers. Expediting cases of emergency would explode the distance, time, and complexity involved in rationing. Could society afford to station an authority at every intersection? Most of the wardens' time would be wasted waiting for a next simultaneous arrival to occur.

Tech

With a capital project, traffic engineers could install utilities and timed stoplights, to ration every crossing. Lamps cost less per hour than mostly idle wardens.

The rule of obeying a red light creates its own issues. Deserted red lights are a solution in search of a problem: They prescribe waiting to no productive end. A pre-scripted timer is informed by neither of the current-state keys at *gemba* that drive waiting waste and collisions—arrivals and departures. Overall waiting loss is still high, plus we added capital, upkeep, and operating costs. Against anarchy we may be tempted to add further complexity of cameras.

Unexpectedly, More Tech for the Tech

We could mitigate some loss at deserted "dumb" lights with more capital and another kind of rule upon the rule: Arrival and departure sensors, with programmable logic. But what is the system to do in a power outage? Increased complexity runs to unintended consequences, and a bureaucratic reflex that multiplies rules for elaborating the rules.

Bifurcation

The evolution of intersections hints at how complex systems *bifurcate*. This means that even a small bump, if the right bump, can send a calm system off into a new pattern, an unintended quantum. Some call this *phase change*. Things jump to resettle toward a *strange attractor*.[10] Michael Crichton made his fortune spinning novels about this kind of surprise (*Andromeda Strain*, *Airframe*, *Jurassic Park*, *Prey*, *State of Fear*, etc.)

Bifurcation in Financial Markets[11]

If you prefer nonfiction, look at market trading: Transaction lag time was historically seen as a value-subtracting frictional barrier to acting on our aims. Windows of opportunity can be fleeting. Traders dreamed about the upside that instantaneous transaction could mean. Then the advent of PCs and program trading turned their science fiction into a millisecond reality.

An unappreciated aspect of frictional delay was that it had always provided space for calm human overseers to dampen volatility. This implicit, negative feedback loop had always harbored the stock exchange from runaways of excess. But we don't see what we can't see.

Computerized trading reconnected buyers and sellers in a new way. It became possible for swings accelerate into runs, quicker than overseers foresaw the need to imagine. The 1987 Wall Street collapse was triggered by the runaway of an algorithmic positive feedback loop. Consequently, regulators instituted computerized "circuit breakers" (rules) to trigger time-outs if sharp runs are detected. This gave humans the possibility to reaffirm and protect system status, in the event of the exceptionally unexpected.

In the years that followed, the rise of derivatives knitted what had been separate markets into a behavioral web, indirect but real. In 2010, one routine algorithmic trade in Kansas set off an avalanche in the indices.

As many as 300 stock prices flickered by 60 percent. Apple flashed from $250 to $100,000 per share. Breakers tripped, so investors could restabilize quickly.

Bifurcation in the Ukraine

Year over year at Chernobyl, layers of added rules accrued in the pursuit of improving safety on the electrical generation side of the plant. The nuclear reactor side also accumulated its own rules, in layers, toward improved safety margin. As Rod Adams relates,

> On April 26th, 1986, at 1:23 am, Alexander Akimov did what he and thousands of other nuclear plant operators have been trained to do. When confronted with confusing reactor indications, he initiated an emergency shutdown of Unit 4.[12]

In one peculiar complex of circumstances this was the worst thing to have done. Shutdown procedure joined the two sides' safety rules into an unforeseeable "perfect storm." Nuclear meltdown was set off by interaction of partners' playbooks for prioritizing safety.

Edward Rutledge

The *Declaration of Independence's* youngest signer was born in Charleston. He studied in London. He became South Carolina's Governor. Goldie Hawn is said to be his descendant. Her daughter, actress Kate Hudson, was born in California, and settled in Colorado. At Rutledge's birth in 1749, no planner could have predicted the string of ironies that would link law school in London, to Federalism in Charleston, to posing in LA, to sons, movies, and the views in Aspen. After the fact, any kid with a web browser can connect the dots.

An Antidote: Epistemic Humility

Hubris twists brilliance of discovery about a system's *parts* into pretense that we understand the system. Expertly knowing the parts, we presume, endows us with ability to bend the whole to our aims. New candidates are made for Darwin Awards, and hilarity ensues.

The surprises of bifurcation are not anomalies, but a universal feature of complex systems. When beneficial we celebrate the windfall. When harmful we call it "act of god" or crash. Positive feedback loops self-reinforce to an attractor, exponentially. Negative feedback loops tend to recoil from loss linearly, and self-stabilize.

Complex systems contain multiple attractor states, not all recognized. We may not perceive some until they school us by veering bent-for-leather down into that unexpected basin of attraction. That our complex system will bifurcate is entirely predictable. When, where, and in what combination, is not possible to forecast. It consists in a universe of permutations. Only in retrospect can critics diagram how every star and planet lined up into a complex misfortune.

This is unsettling. First reaction is to try to plan away any possibility of getting blind-sided. It runs to cosmic whack-a-mole—the expensive, bureaucratic vanity of "do something." Or scapegoating because "you get paid to own it, and somebody should have known." Who is to say a mode we know about will be the one (of many) to trigger the big event? To expect bifurcation is not fatalism, no suggestion to avoid atoms, derivatives, or other forms that progress takes. The lesson is to stay always mindful of our need for ***epistemic humility***.

Epistemic means how do we know that we *know*. Humility is not surrender—it is having the spine to admit to finite limits on what we can control and to prepare in that light. *Epistemic humility* does plan, on the assumption that we won't foresee every strange attractor.

This ought not stymie enterprise (a French word for trying and discovery). Part of our plan is that the unintended can pay a visit and override any cognitive intent. Like Mike Tyson said, *everybody has a plan 'til they get punched in the mouth.*

Complex systems consist of three components: *stocks, flows, and feedback loops.* Feedback is iterative adaptation, not the firing-and-forgetting of one-way directives. We engineer situations that on balance promote emergence on beneficial attractors. Then we lead as learners, that is, recovering knowers. As setbacks manifest we reflect deeply, adapt the rule-set with mutuality on the new learning, and realign on next steps forward. We learn to expect, absorb, mitigate, and exploit even what we suffer to learn from bifurcation, to propel us forward. As John Miller put it:

> that we might create complex systems that do only good is a delusion. That said, complex systems that work well provide so many benefits that we [should be] willing to accept some occasional failures.

> When complexity abounds, there be dragons.[13]

This returns us to the question of rules for an effective intersection:

The Traffic Circle

Circles emerged as a simple, effective counter against waiting, cost, and hazards of crossing.

Two drivers in Durango, CO, enter the circle at the same time. Separate aims mutually self-order without delay.

On just a few rules, in varying circumstances of arrival and departure, the circle wordlessly forms up mutual allocation, for less waste than the rule-sets we compared earlier. It has lower capital cost. If so much traffic forms up that stoppages persist, we need only widen the lanes to hold the flux. This self-ordering system runs at no expense for utilities, sensors, or wardens. It just unbreakably, simply works. What rules are needed?

- Enter counterclockwise (right) into the circle.
- Yield to traffic from left. Where there is a gap, proceed without stopping.
- No stopping in the circle. Go around to your destination pointer. Exit right.
- If you miss a turn, relax and take a lap.

In the late 1900s, "scientific management" displaced most of these in favor of sensors, lights, and prescriptive programming. Since then technocracy has run a tired course, and circles are staging a comeback.

Emergence—a Great Architect

In complex systems, the manner in which we agree to connect is premeditated. **The rule-set shapes *how* the system will join up the inputs, should interactions come to pass.**

Interactions that arise out of individuals' own independent pursuits cause auto assembly of +1 levels, **greater spans of order that were no product of the actors' design or intent**. Here precisely is the mechanism why the lean practices work.

Hanging around at a visual replenishment pull rack and just watching the adaptive rearrangement continually re-form itself without a conductor is a spectacle of order that rivals the intricacy of an opera or ballet. Extended order is a resultant fallout of the simple rule-set.

Another illustration is how search-engine rankings form up when a product comes to the Internet. There are uncountable paths to any web address. Some become famous and well-trodden. Most never happen once. Similar trails form when a building, wilderness, or industrial park opens. First time out, everyone comes up with what seems a reasonable path.

Within days, intricate patterns of order form up, without a directing mastermind. That a path got taken before means some tall grass is trampled, thorns bent, initial search rankings built. Some paths are eased, a cue inviting further use and improvement. Some ways get harder, with barriers, signs, fences, and congestion emerging where too many others got the same idea. The same universe of possible ways still exists. Where individual learnings interact, they join in complex. Certain kinds of pathways self-assemble into things unexpectedly better.

Planners poured sidewalks before the grand opening. Some will end up getting used as predicted, some will idle away, and some will be repurposed in an aha moment. "Keep Off Grass" signs will pop up where actual users realize shortcuts unforeseen when the campus was formed in the dreams of distant developers. As Hayek pointed out, the attractors embodied in a rule-set are what radiate the fundamental drawing force that lean calls "pull":

> Human movements through the region come to conform to a definite pattern which, **although the result of deliberate decisions of many people, has yet not been consciously designed by anyone.**[14]

So, in your enterprise are we going to stay off the grass, or not?

CHAPTER 3

Lean Uses Emergence to Extend Order

Civilization advances by extending the number of important operations which we can perform without thinking about them. Operations of thought are like cavalry charges in a battle – they are strictly limited in number; they require fresh horses, and must only be made at decisive moments.[1]

—A. N. Whitehead

Reflexive versus Cognitive Tactics

We affect and are affected by many others, in conduct of departmental and personal aims. We choose to forego instant gratification, untrained impulse, selfishness, tribalism, and *hubris*. We subscribe to composed manners to connect. Our intersections are guided on *non-instinctual, abstract, mutual* rules. Where this behavior prevails, novel rearrangements emerge among the actors and extend system gain to fresh levels. This is the age-old, reliable, way to progress.

A rule-set is the sweat-equity saved up out of hard work, reflection, chickens-come-home-to-roost, fortunate-accidental discoveries, and analysis. It fences out behaviors that don't end well. It up-fits the structural stability of groups. It is the essence of kinds of conditions that we have learned promote mutuality, ingenuity, and gain.

What we don't know often outnumbers the knowns. Circumstance is fleeting, so what constitutes the "right" action now is fleeting. Because interactions are unplanned, doesn't mean they must be un-scripted.

Louis Pasteur said, "fortune favors the prepared mind." We can't say what circumstances will happen today. But learners develop a pretty good idea which *kinds* of circumstances are likely. Some situations are so critical that even if they are unlikely, we ought to be prepared for them.

Lean is about getting ready to *act like we've been there before*. Reflexive methods hold great advantage over command-control, in the conduct of tactics. Lean fashions devices that use the work itself to project the rule-set. We set up routine operation so that it implicitly points out to the actors their best way to coordinate in the circumstance. A well-designed system projects the incentive to heed the advice being signaled.

Looking back, time dims what were the suppositions and reasons behind today's rules. The social contract bound up in "standard" does not have to be just archived in an expert's library. It can be made part of the signaling that we get the process to emit. We don't leave those coming on board now to imagine why things were put this way: The system keeps the bargain out on display. This transcends sociological fault lines. Operating signals point out why it is mutual to uphold costly lessons.

Looking ahead, to do the *go-see* loop is to solicit *loyal opposition*. It institutionalizes users' questioning how "standard" might be adapted to serve better. It promotes amendment over avoidance, procrastination, cherry-picking the parts of "standard" we do and don't like, or revolt when a norm has grown intolerable.

Lean simplifies the grasp of what is going on. Of the range of action open to us, we reflexively recognize the combo that maximizes mutuality in how to allocate contested resources. It renders abstract relations tangible and unambiguous, reducing uncertainty and distrust. It brings efficiency of inter-*personal*, inter-*spatial*, and inter-*temporal* transmission of information among stakeholders, across the extended order.

Tactical triggers and directional pointers call up reflex, rather than dialing up out-of-cycle expert intervention. So, reflexive runs orders of magnitude better than cognitive direction, in speed, repeatability, signal-to-noise, and error-proofing.

Some say lean could have been called "in-your-face": The default is to *not* push issues out of the *gemba* to third parties. Reflex escalates the folks on the spot. If the right ones are not on the spot it pulls them to it (usually by causing flow to stop). If "Is" doesn't equal "Ought," action is obliged:

Where the issue is management-controllable, it sets leaders to either fix standard, or fix our failure to resource per the standard. Where the issue is operator-controllable, it puts front liners on the hook to address cause (not blame) for not executing to "standard."

Reflex generates *system pressure* to fix causes (not hush symptoms with pacifiers—inventory, excess capacity, or making customers wait).

Visuality of the lean practices decouples sending from receiving of feedback on how processes are doing at their linkages. This liberates customer and supplier to go patrol a span, not tied down by need to stay waiting physically on one spot in case of outage.

The Upshot

- Cognitive planning focuses on the extent of compliance it can institute. It looks to expertise to reconcile abstract resourcing issues and choices, off-line, by analysis.
- Reflexive focuses on extent of peer-to-peer mutual initiative it can induce. It looks to cues and signals to reconcile abstract resourcing issues and choices, on the spot.

R.C. Sproul advised *simplicity without being so simplistic as to distort the message*. Lean renders abstract operational rules trainable, retainable, persuasive as to value in following the guidance.

Lean Exploits Reflex at Four Levels

First order	Managing workplace	Process resourcing
Second order	How workplaces interact	Process connection
Third order	Flow	System rate of connection
Fourth order	Improvement of the system	Rate of change of the system

First Order: Managing Workplace (Process resourcing)

In *5 Pillars of the Visual Workplace* Hiroyuki Hirano set out the use of visuality in a formula, 5S: Sort, Straighten, Shine, Standardize, Sustain. Note what his fifth S stands for.

Hirano focused on how to deploy (S1→S4). The how and why of S5 are mostly left to the student to flesh out. Advocates continue to publish numerous how-to-5S guides. Sustain is always acknowledged as a priority, then almost always left to the shortest chapter.

No one questions the ought-to of sustain. Anyone who has done visual management (not cosmetics) knows that holding the gains is a big deal. What has been lacking is a well-referenced, detailed why. Learners struggling to change their culture in a lasting way have awaited in-depth resources to underpin the how, and win their cultures over to the whys. This missing link was a major motivation for the writing of this book.

Somewhere along the way, 5S started being marketed like a credential, a trendy flavor, a productivity event. Canned, event-based rollouts have conditioned frontline recipients of the outside attention to cope by externalism, compliance, and housekeeping. 5S done *to*—not *for*— the affected is lean theater. Many corporatized initiatives entirely miss the point.

Like kittens and puppies, who could be "against" 5S? But those accountable to deliver operating results ask for justification of the cost and interruption. It is a reasonable question. Too often, we meet them with platitudes, *if you build it they will come*. "Because 5S" is not a reason.

5S is no potion that transmutes tidiness magically into quality, delivery, or payback. It is an expensive prop, if done from the motive of signaling leader virtues, or to polish the brand. Lean that isn't theater runs to a higher standard. Justifiable 5S is done on a clear proposition: *Clean to inspect, inspect to detect, detect to correct, correct to perfect.*

5S exposes problems. Cosmetics and housekeeping are incidental outcomes, untenable motives. 5S makes no claim to solve what it brings to light. How to triage and handle the exposed is a separate matter. We will pick back up on this in later chapters.

This reformed image of 5S offers an explicit, falsifiable value proposition that goes to gap exposure, not optics. It is about gaining early warning on our prospects for meeting expectations, in view of the current status of resourcing.

Gwendolyn Galsworth perfectly captures 5S as the principle of *visuality*—endowing complex, mute operations with *a voice from the physical world.*[2]

To achieve standard, doers require not just indiscriminate lots of "stuff". They require specific materials, tools, and information. For services to provide other/more/less than specifically this, is the bell-cow for non-attainment.[3] We may not see it yet, but we can hear it coming. The advantages of visuality are many:

- It is efficient. Simple, error-proofed coordination self-organizes without the expense, distortion, and lag of narratives, meetings, and directors.
- This tide raises all societal boats. Signals and cues are unaffected by accent, credentials, looks, ancestry, or whatever. 5S expresses gaps, opportunities, and windfalls in stimuli that are intuitive and **self-announcing** to any who tries to contribute.
- 5S doesn't wait for specialists. It points up spontaneous, contextual response. It counters the primary cause of interruption—**information deficits**.

Its deliverable is to visually broadcast the status of resourcing gaps: *What is needed, where*, in specific *quantity, condition, presentation*, and *when*. Passive cues stand current resourcing up in contrast to target condition (how it ought to be). Deviations **self-report**. Waffle House has built an ROI empire on this simplicity.[4]

5S is a method for emergence called *stigmergy*.[5] *That means, it embeds the information actors operate on, into the workplace or workpiece itself.* Passive cues align and allocate the abstract web of contributors, for zero supervisory cost. It eliminates the cost of pulling out of cycle to analyze, narrate, or direct traffic around outages.

Lean borrows 5S straight out of nature. All manner of plants and animals use gestures, songs, scents, shapes, colors, trails, and other such devices. Nature signals in this way to implicitly broadcast target condition, actual status, correctives, and complex allocations. Human operations can exploit the same tricks to align extended orders of contributors, for minimal overhead.

Cues guide us onto acts that promote extension of order. Visuality yells at passers-by, *here's what you need to know; here's what you need to share.* As Hayek put it,

Order is desirable not for keeping everything in its place, but for generating new powers that would otherwise not exist.[6]

5S Example: Shadowboard for Station A Tools

Shadowboards announce the availability of prescribed tools, in effective quantity and usable presentation. Anyone can see what is supposed to be where (rule). *Visuality* means not pushing the value-adding actors out of cycle, into excess motion, transport, and waiting wastes (hunting, fetching, asking, and explaining).

Round 1

Station A needs three specific tools, to deliver as expected: two mallets— not three, not zero. They need one specific wrench. Hatching is exposed if a standard item is missing. Extras self-report. With no home, their presence creates a visual deviation.

Standard is a hypothesis of what users need, to meet expectation safely, with quality, on time, productively. Operating is an experimental check of standard against reality.

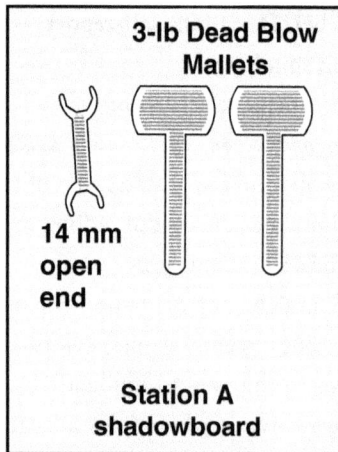

In this world's long history, reality is undefeated. We don't have to wait for workers to miss plan, to know that support is lacking. On a proactive cadence, wise leaders *go-see* to it that value producers have what they need.

Round 2

Does "Is" match "Ought"? *Listen to the voice from the physical world.* Any tool that belongs has home location marked on it. This provides for self-explanatory **recoil** to its home.

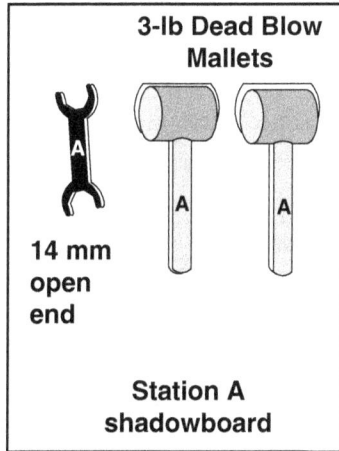

All needed tools are here. Move on: We have other stations to check in rounds.

Round 3

Now here is a problem. Even passers-by get visually notified, three-fold:

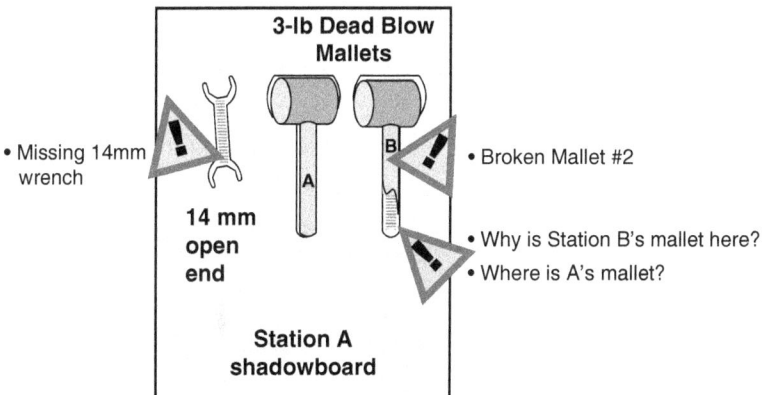

We thought that we had provided what the users need. So, the appearance of these gaps between actual and standard herald something we should know, but didn't yet. Any concerned party can see the problem, without reports or experts. The only ones who need be interrupted are those responsible to come recover and follow up on causes.

If these means are required, Station **A** is not going to meet standard. This notice gives a chance to intervene before cause can run too far ahead of capacity to recover. If despite this outage **A** does hit standard, why does the board show these as necessary? Reality may be schooling what we thought we knew about this operation.

5S at **A** shows that **B** has its own issues. Whoever got **A**'s mallet has their own issues, too. We will *go-see*, not wait to miss plan. Servant leaders fetch missing resources. With the affected, we go seek out reasons why, to improve the system itself for the future.

Second Order: How Workplaces Interact (Process connection)

Consider sequential but separated processes. We link them together to complete a service.

Candidates arrive at Step 1. It does its thing, as the "supplier" of WIP to "customer," Step 2. Step 2 does its thing as "customer" of Step 1 but "supplier" to Step 3. Step 3 receives WIP and translates it into finished goods for an end-customer.

In the case of a hiring queue, work-in-process (WIP) is neighbors needing work. Waiting subtracts value. They could be searching elsewhere if here is not a fit. We could spend more time training, if tied up less with ones who don't join. It is mutuality to connect in a way that minimizes wait and increases speed.

Let's survey and contrast the ways firms commonly connect steps.

Example: Typical Process Connection—Use of Unregulated Inventory

Most operations default to *unregulated inventory* to connect sequential steps.

This form of connection leaves high degrees of freedom. A job comes in the door. Eventually it gets pressed out the back door by the in-flow of arrivals behind it, and some resultant of many internal collisions.

Here is **push** – speculative overproduction.

Customer process has not signaled a need yet for next candidate. Still, here come the masses.

Push into overflow compels next stage to take what they don't yet need. This is not mutuality.

WIP Cap between stages is nonexistent. There is no discernible sequence

Self-order ceases, queues back up, entropy sets in.

Register

Interview

Check-out

There is room between steps, so a variable lot of new stuff can swell up inside the building without anything necessarily getting pressed out the back door to a customer. WIP waits more than moves, in this system. Steps are tied loosely by the variable accumulation of WIP between them. Throughput time is ad hoc and highly variable. This brings us to a definition:

In **Push**, completion at my step is what authorizes me to press WIP forward to the next.

The force that impels flow of jobs through system comes from upstream processes sending WIP forward, whether a customer process is ready, and asks for it, or not.

In systems tied together by unregulated inventory, suppliers push out WIP, decoupled from whether next steps use it forward or not. On a Value Stream Map, it looks like this:

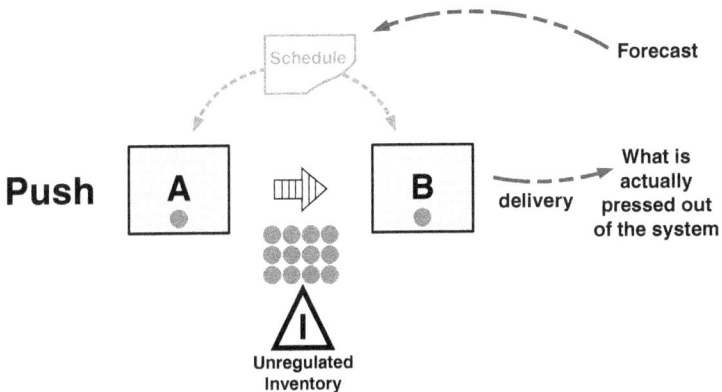

Schedule

Forecast

Push A   B

delivery

What is actually pressed out of the system

Unregulated Inventory

This system has **stocks** and **flows**, but **no feedback loop** to be found. It is complex alright, but this is no complex *adaptive* system. On our best day, its upside is linear. But issues can back its queues up exponentially. Downside is asymmetric over upside.

Unregulated inventory is the brute force way to bind steps into a system and cause passage of work through it. It is like pushing a rope. Only the foolishly rich can absorb so low an output relative to the stock of resources balled up between the internal steps. Work let in the front door is barely coupled to what paying customers are waiting for us to send out the back.

Example: Connect Arrivals to Our In-House Process, with Simple Kanban

A *kanban* is a cue that imposes a designed manner how we permit joined steps to interact. It can arrange a fluctuating stream of arrivals, whose processing times vary, into a systematic form of movement through the system, with mutuality and efficiency.

In *kanban*, customer use of WIP they have is what authorizes us to deliver a next one.

User returns a simple (normally visual) cue back upstream to supplier. For instance, they can send a card saying what they used up. Or they could return their used containers, to cue refill. It is the user who triggers WIP. This minimizes and levels the time WIP sits waiting between steps.

Consider the hiring example. If we allow a surged lobby to overflow applicants into the internal workings of Register-Interview-Checkout, it will increase everyone's wait.

- The disorder of multiple persons vying to be attended interrupts the servers. Time spent on interruption is time spent not processing the backlog.
- It lures service providers into the fallacy of "multitasking." This increases the percentage of time wasted on "switching cost". Switchtasking is not the same as execution of tasks. It is a deceptive waste because it makes busy people feel "efficient."

Kanban adaptively cues and pulls actors in line with the attractor of mutuality and velocity. We can express this in a basic rule-set:

> Internal steps will process applicants one at a time. This minimizes
>   lost time, and maximizes speed at which everyone is handled fairly.
> Lobby arrivals join into the hiring process, using a blue *kanban* square.
> When the square goes empty, this cue pulls the next applicant forward
>   to **Register**.
> Only one advances into the square at a time.

Squares and arrows embedded in the workplace make bounds of mutual action visual. The intended attractor translates into a simple rule-set, which we arrange into visual cues anyone can do. Any stakeholder can start imagining ways to try to improve on it.

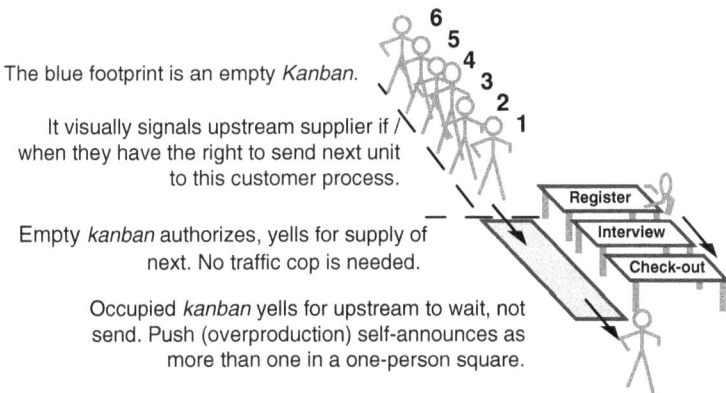

The blue footprint is an empty *Kanban*.

It visually signals upstream supplier if / when they have the right to send next unit to this customer process.

Empty *kanban* authorizes, yells for supply of next. No traffic cop is needed.

Occupied *kanban* yells for upstream to wait, not send. Push (overproduction) self-announces as more than one in a one-person square.

Register

Interview

Check-out

Where a cue self-explains, and actors conform to the mutuality embodied in it, resources self-arrange toward the basin of attraction.

Good visuals stand up "Is" versus "Ought" in a contrast that can't be missed. No matter how demand may peak and wane, arrivals will always see adaptive advice on a heading of least waiting—no director needed. **Issues self-report.**

If standard turns out to be not as self-explanatory as we thought, it will manifest in visible outage or violating the lines. Where our cues produce surprise, or fail to induce the intent of flow, all can see and wonder why. This puts benevolent system pressure not just on operators, but on the standard itself.

This is an abstract way to relate suppliers to users. For global optimum, actors submit to rules for reasons they may not feel. For instance, *kanban* may throttle a speedy operation to run below its top speed. Still, the guidance of *kanban* remains simple.

Our hiring example no longer consists of just **stocks** and **flows**: We have added a **feedback loop** onto the system, by having arrivals check and act upon the fill-status of *kanban*. Waiting and variability are much reduced. This feedback generates a motive force called **pull**. It impels actors through the process economically, mutually optimizing the resources required to do so.

By making rules and feedback visual, the very use of a system turns the minds of users and providers onto novel rearrangements. It gives the eye-opening illusion of effect preceding cause—of beating the Second Law. How rules might creatively evolve to mutual gain suggests itself to any who *go-see*. Arrivals *kanban* turned hiring from a complex scrum into a complex *adaptive* system.

The Powerful Concept of Pull

The mathematical and financial ideal is to process one piece at a time. On a Value Stream Map, it would look something like this:

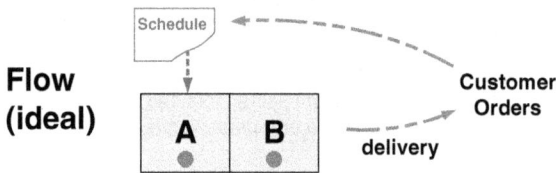

Typically, we discover roadblocks on the first try of this principle. We join the steps together and attempt one piece at a time. "Detractors" (geographical separations, differing process rates, setups, etc.) interrupt delivery often enough to put the ideal out of reach, for now.

This gap between what we ought and what we actually can do on the existing layout leads us to the abstract, complex value proposition of **pull**:

> Aside from how much Standard WIP (SWIP) a system holds, a pull system perfectly mimics the dynamics and economics [marginal cost − marginal revenue] of flow, once wetted. Just like flow, it queues

exponentially better than steps joined by brute push (expediting reactively, unregulated inventory proactively). Even with the detractors, velocity and flexibility to drop-ins improve radically. This calls up another definition:

"**Pull**" means suppliers send forward to next step because the customer signaled demand. Authorization to process a next unit is if, and only if, a paying customer concretely orders it. There is nothing speculative about it. Users call forward what they want, for when (not before or after), in condition and quantity they want.

For pull to mimic the dynamics of one-piece flow, there are *conditions* to be met:

1. WIP between steps must be capped ("blocking")
2. Sequence is conserved

These are the primary levers an operations manager has on economics and delivery.

If all that sounded complex, that's because *it is*. This abstraction frustrates readers. The abstraction turns plenty tangible, when we pay bills and account for time in queue. At appraisal, your lean coordinator will smile and admit it was like shooting fish in a barrel. Pull works every time it is tried, for hundreds or thousands of percentage in ROI.

On a Value Stream Map, the pull arrangement looks something like this:

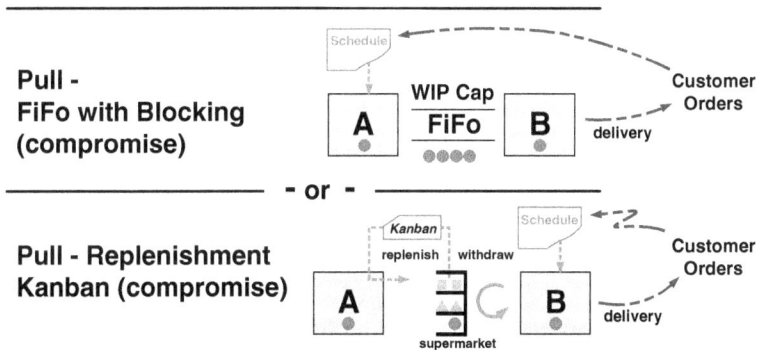

Pull -
FiFo with Blocking
(compromise)

Schedule
WIP Cap
A FiFo B delivery
Customer Orders

- or -

Pull - Replenishment
Kanban (compromise)

Kanban
replenish | withdraw
Schedule
A [supermarket] B delivery
Customer Orders

One way to link customer and supplier processes by the attractor of pull is to use simple *kanban* to visually cue the rule-governed withdrawal and **replenishment** of a **supermarket**.

Alternatively, we can use **FiFo** (first in—first out, to conserve sequence) **with a WIP cap**, as a visual device to connect sequential work steps with a pulling action.

Which to use depends on technicalities of the demand relative to our process. That is a conversation for another time. The point is, simple visuals generate a force that intuitively impels all actors into pull's abstract basin of attraction. Anyone who will just *go-see* can spot ideas and concerns to help adapt the system toward further gain.

Example: Connect Internal Steps with Kanban for Replenishment Pull

In the foregoing, we used *kanban* to pull arrivals into the hiring process. Now let's extend the principle of pull to join the internal steps to one another and to the external demand. *Kanban* is an easy way to pull applicants through Receive-Interview-Checkout, on the attractor of mutuality and speed. Here it is in a basic rule-set:

> Arrivals join into the hiring process, using *kanban* squares in the lobby.
> An empty square pulls the next applicant forward.
> Only one person into a square at a time.
> **Register** assures not less than one, no more than two on deck to **Interview**. (WIP cap)
> **Interview** assures not less than one, no more than two on deck to **Check-out**. (WIP cap)

This will absorb surges and avoid processing outages, while minimizing time in process, snarls, and the waste of "multitasking."

Squares and arrows embedded in the workplace make bounds of action visual. The attractor is translated into a rule-set, arranged as cues anyone can do and imagine how to improve.

In this system, our pull prerequisites get visually watch-dogged by *kanban*.

At each customer-supplier interface we visually prescribe target condition – connection behavior.

Rule Set: Empty = Send. Full = Stop Sending.

Candidates self-organize to hold sequence and WIP Cap.

Register

Interview

Check-out

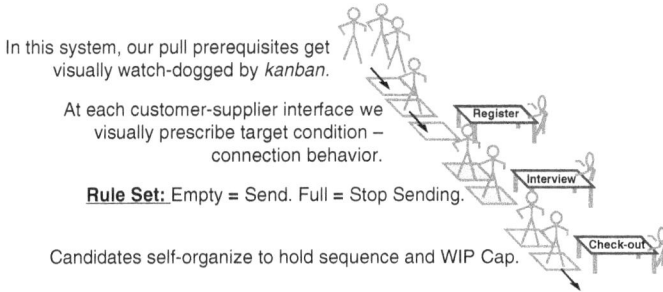

About Electronic Kanban

Some planners relegate replenishment to computers. Transaction errors tip electronic *kanban* into push behavior, in actual queues at the units.

Can electronic reorder cap WIP and keep sequence at a queue? With intentional scanning logic, yes. But if the prerequisites are neglected, cosmetic "pull" devolves into glorified digital push. Directors who don't *go-see*, wonder why.

Visual replenishment is simple with *kanban* to guide actors on appropriate next action. It uses *stigmergy*. Any uninvited deviance into push self-reports. Broken sequence self-reports: If we step over lines it shows. Respect of WIP cap is self-evident. Correctives can self-assemble.

Reasons may lie out of cycle for the locals, but system flow rapidly recovers. If reasons are captured, system pressure builds to nudge stakeholders to come help amend the rules.

In transience, order is a harbor of stable expectations. Rules shelter fragile cooperation from caprice and coercion, randomness, variability, and novelty or closed-minded conservatism for its own sake. Fledgling order can calmly form, correct, and extend itself. Participants can step forward in the fog of a moment: They are sheltered by persuasion that the signals along compass heading of the rule-set equate to advancing their mutual interests.

Third Order: Flow (System rate of connection)

Example: Shared Process—Serves Multiple Feeds in, or Types Outbound

Sharing binds supplier and customer processes in a complexity that is one exponent up from a straight linkage. That's because multiple suppliers interact not only with the customer but with one another too. Though parts of a single plan, the streams are *rivalrous*: Any one's use of the shared process delays the others. If there is a burp, queues blow up exponentially, not linearly.

For example, consider a saw that trims jobs from five feeders. Some run fast, with no setup. Others need big setups. Some run slowly. Some arrive in big batches. Or consider a customs agent who serves arrivals inbound from multiple origins, outbound to separate baggage rechecks.

Setups equal not running while impatient lines grow. Expediting is an unthinking reflex. We see *gaming behavior* (some jobs re-classed "Hot"). Actors batch their demand, to reduce the number (time) of setups they must perform. These are understandable but self-defeating outbreaks of push. Uncontrolled WIP backs up.

Leaders relent on cap rules to allow upstream suppliers to keep sending, for "efficiency." Rushes are privileged over the others and bump to the front. The rest in line, get double-handled to make way. Sequence is scrambled. Those who don't get put to the front of the line know it and resent it. Mutuality is undercut. The service providers have to negotiate a confliction of hot lists and multiple schedules. All these poor actors need a *kata* to reflexively self-arrange themselves and their shared resource, toward mutual extension of order, on the spot.

How Do You Spell Relief? E–P–E–I

Aggregate wait would minimize if we allocated timeshares on the quickest doable cycle through mean demand quantity of the families, in rotating sequence. This optimal cadence is called **EPEI** (Each Part Every Interval).

The above prescription is abstract. It was hard to write. It is admittedly hard for a hurried reader to read. Be that as it may, it is in their enlightened interest to cowboy up and try. We all suffer poorly managed shared processes. With the aid of *stigmergy*, lean transforms EPEI into practical relief to millions of the deserving weary.

It mitigates a pooled queue by $\sqrt{}$ square root of number of families. It levels out spikes in arrivals of hot families, fairly. Rivals re-form back into mutuality, so long as it stays open and fair. Trust earns, gaming eases, batch sizes relax, and when frequent, small deliveries are deemed reliable.

Some days the EPEI rule may direct one family to pull off before running through the whole of a spike. On other days the shared resource may be adaptively guided to wrap up early on that family. It evens out. Medium term, the collaborators review and update the EPEI shares, if needed to adapt to change in demand. Mutual adaptation upholds trust.

Lot Formation

To create pull, we arrange the workspace to segregate arrivals by family. Intrafamily, the arrival sequence is kept. Interfamily rivals must voluntarily await their calculated turns, like sequenced slices of a pie. **This sounds complicated, because it is.**

We tame complexity only by rigorously upholding rules of pull and mutuality. If we stick to principle over temptation, EPEI delivers—but in a pretty abstract way. How might we package this, to uphold *the consent of the governed* under the dynamics of pressure?

Command-control won't uphold persuasion when an enforcer is not watching. Re-explaining daily with pep talks and recalculation can't keep up real-time, across a full sociological span.

We need a simple, strict, self-arranging way to package the cap-sequence. We need it self-explanatory so anyone intuitively sees what to do, persuaded to stay on the pointed heading.

We turn to the elegant simplicity of *stigmergy*. A visual *heijunka* (leveling) box symbolically depicts how the **rates** of interacting processes should connect, for EPEI pull, not push.

Example: Leveling (heijunka) Box

Make a box whose volume depicts the capacity of the shared process being leveled: Face area literally depicts time available on the asset.

To make timeshare intuitive, subdivide in increments of time relative to pitch of the processes feeding into and serving out of it. Dimension the face area of the box overall to one EPEI cycle worth of job routers, in size. Use this box to display the planned operating sequence, holding the job tickets we are advised to process, in order.

For example, say EPEI is 1 day. Set up a box to hold that many routers.

Typical lots in/out use 5 to 45-minute runtime. A 1-hour increment is fine to see how things are tracking versus plan, through the shift.

Mean demand: 8 hours of A, 3 hours B, 2 hours C, 2 hours D, 1 hour E.

Reserve 1 hour for walk-ins, end of first shift. These earn a premium.

Curing tank demands 7-hour deep cleaning every day. Do it on the third shift.

We don't deal today's work out in an un-discriminated bucket. The process is:

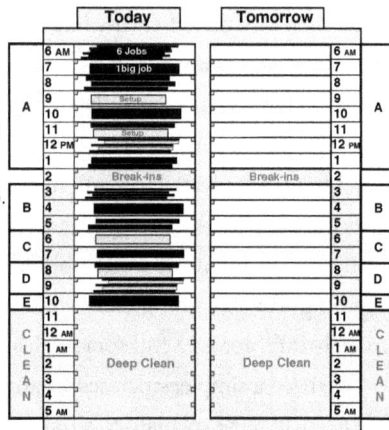

Sort yesterday's arrivals by family.

Keep sequence within family.

Parse jobs from each family into Today side of box, up to the EPEI share of time.

We can see respect of pull (Cap, sequence).

1-hr intervals render the sequence check-able.

Stakeholders Come-See, on cadence. It keeps peace among potential rivals.

Visuality self-announces when variation throws unexpected wrinkles like interruptions or over/under-capacity

If more arrivals show up than can fit into "Tomorrow," the box presents a literal, visual display of push. It may be due to just daily variability. Or it may be advance notice of something more. Each day we will keep sequence: First we absorb holdovers from the prior day. Then go on with the arrivals since, in sequence.

The box is sized to level the *average* demand, so about half the time a day's arrivals will be less than the size of a day's box. Half the time arrivals will overflow a day-sized box. It should even out over a couple of days.

If a backlog persists, it is that voice from the physical world, urging that we revisit our notion of "average" demand. Perhaps mix or overall demand shifted enough to recalculate the timeshare.

Similar reasoning applies if under-fill persists. We may need to re-level by updating EPEI and reallocating idle resources. Visuality calls out to all the stakeholders to start getting curious about the emerging question. We can deal with things while they are still small.

Example: Go to *Gemba as Scheduled, at 10:00 a.m.*

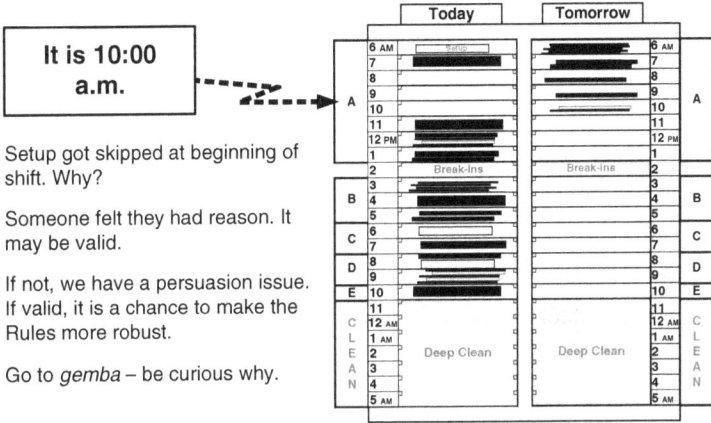

It is 10:00
a.m.

Setup got skipped at beginning of
shift. Why?

Someone felt they had reason. It
may be valid.

If not, we have a persuasion issue.
If valid, it is a chance to make the
Rules more robust.

Go to *gemba* – be curious why.

Example: Go to *Gemba as Scheduled, at 1:30 p.m.*

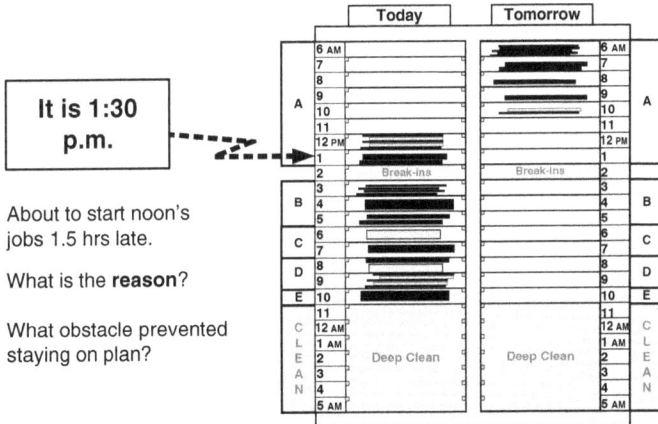

It is 1:30
p.m.

About to start noon's
jobs 1.5 hrs late.

What is the **reason**?

What obstacle prevented
staying on plan?

EPEI in a leveling box is an elegant, simple way to visualize a complex, abstract rule-set. It links customer–supplier processes in dynamic, adaptive mutuality, real-time, on the spot.

Fourth Order: Improvement of the System (Rate of change of system)

Cross-line implementation and **recombinance** are examples of ways to apply emergence to improve the system itself. We should acknowledge that, as nonnegotiable as these should be, they require a level of abstraction that most do not do. Among those who do, few do so visually. Depicting higher abstraction, simply, is hard. As Blaise Pascal put it, *I would have written you a shorter letter but I didn't have time.*

Without visuality, big propositions are naked before sustainment's detractors. Complex schemes become the province of "belts" and authority. We ask the normals to hold to rules they don't grasp. Mutuality frays. Specialists do compliance to workers, in place of discovery with them.

Technicality is only half the challenge. We must keep in public view the value in improving the system itself. Failure to be simple and adaptive opens the door to misapplication of tools. It is incumbent on leaders (OpEx doubly) to render improvement *simple, not simplistic and distorted.*

Example: Cross-Training Matrix

The matrix displays how cross-trained the locals are on the array of functions that comprise a unit's task. It is a picture of how qualified they are to flex.

To turn novices loose before validating would disrespect them and the customers who receive their product. The matrix lets us confirm that workers are not pushed into positions affecting others in ways they can't (yet) support with competence.

⊕	New	Restricted from Performing This Function, Task, or releasing product or service to next step in process	Competency Profile
⊕	Aware Train Only	Grasps Key Points - product, job steps key to Safety, Compliance, Quality, Delivery, Cost. Recognizes, can escalate (block for review of questionable). Restricted - may not release work to next step without trainer verification.	from novice,
⊕	Restricted Operation	Validated, released to perform some of the Duties. Not yet validated in other Duties. Scheduled to train in, Restricted from the not-yet validated duties. Does not yet perform at customer demand rate (Takt)	to restricted practitioner,
⊕	Unrestricted Operation	Validated SCQDC to all Job Duties of the position. Released to operate without Restriction, at customer demand Rate (Takt)	to full practitioner,
⊕	Trainer	Can perform all Job Duties at Takt; Can train others into competency in the job; Can counter-verify product, the work, and trainees in key points at Takt (both knowledge and demonstrated skills)	to trainer.

Consider an appliance line with three production roles:

A—Subassembly and Piping,
B—Welding and Wiring,
C—Testing and Wrap-up

We don't need to read HR files to verify qualification. We *go-see* on the spot. The matrix shows who is released for what. If restrictions apply, those are clear. We see who is in the job. "Is" versus "Ought" self-announces. There is no information deficit, so there is no interruption.

Certifications like ISO don't need to be as paper-intensive as we have done. The training matrix is first-order (5S) *stigmergy* on a rule to protect customers from unqualified work.

In our example, Piping and Wiring show NO qualified workers. Yet we are sending out units. Breach of trust self-announces. This escalates, generating system pressure.

	Header Subassemble	Circuit Subassemble	Piping 1	Piping 2	Welding	Panel Wiring	Unit Wiring	Mechanical Testing	Electrical Testing	Skin	
Susan Koger	◔	◔	⊕ 3/2	3/13		⊕	⊕ 5/3	⊕			◀ Date to Qualify
Raja Kumar				⊕	◔	⊕ 3/2	⊕ 3/13	⊕			◀ Date to Qualify
Brieon Archer	◔	◔	⊕ 5/1	⊕ 3/13				◔	◔	◔	◀ Date to Qualify
Matt Wynn					◔	⊕ 3/2	⊕ 3/13	◔	◔	◔	◀ Date to Qualify
	Operation A				Op. B			Op. C			

Next, we can add "Date to Qualify" to this matrix, to take it to the fourth order: It now visually lays out the strategic intent and rate to improve the system itself.

In this example, that means creating the cross-training and staffing to support the sales we committed to. This is providing for the means, not just demanding the outcomes of a strategy. File this away for our discussions on *hoshin* (strategic alignment).

A going concern balances exploitation and exploration. Firms that only exploit existing business go obsolete. Firms that do nothing but explore, and don't execute on it, starve.

Recombinance schemes like **cross-line implementation** are the primary mode of successful exploration in nature and enterprise. The birds and bees somehow know and do it: Recombinance is cross-pollination, grafting splices of success onto new domains.

It is not done because we know ahead what it will yield. It is the intentional bumping of the complex system, to see what learning arises out of the perturbation. System restabilizes to attractor. Optima emerge, which point us to unexpected new outcomes.

Recombinance is among the powerful forces, the *deep structures* of the earth: It is the workhorse of genetic advance. But in the details, it is high mathematics. How might we render it to the participation of the common persons in the value stream?

Example: Evolutionary Operation

EVOP is visual management for recombinant tuning of process settings. For the chemical engineers, Box and Draper spelled out the principle like this:

> It is inefficient to run an industrial process in such a way that only a product is produced . . . a process should be operated so as to produce . . . also information on how to improve.[7]

EVOP is statistical exploration by deliberate excursions in process setpoints, around the center point of standard conditions. A simple visual called a *sputnik* guides workers through a random sequence of recombinant tries.

Observation by observation, operators collect a picture of the complex output of the plant, called a response surface.

In conventional Designed Experimentation, specialists come and probe the process with large bumps, to provoke easily confirmed outcomes, on minimal sample size.

In EVOP, workers bide their time, with repeats of tiny bumps. What these lack in amplitude, they make up in sample size.

Eventually a picture forms - advice to next incremental step on a patient journey of continuous improvement.

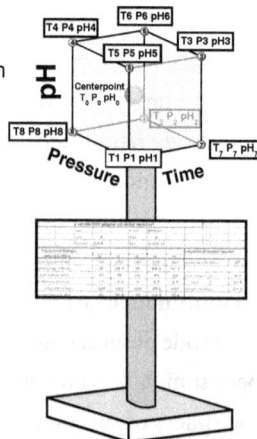

EVOP doesn't interrupt delivery and revenue with disruptive trials. It learns through steady repetition of fractional-factorial design while producing salable goods. Facilitators regularly bring lacking resources, remove obstacles, and mutually confirm next steps based on rounds of guidance the frontline workers self-assembled.

Blue collar operators have done this without computers since the 1950s. The elegance, social power, and economics of this visual sort of recombinant exploration are stunning.

Michelin's Leadership Development

Name a university or people group—Michelin likely employs it. It is a case study in viewpoint and background diversity, and it shows up in discoveries decade after decade. At Normandy on D-Day, Michelin maps guided the troops. It gave the world the first paved runway, developed warplanes, and invented the car jack and radial tires. Since long ago it can guarantee truck tire casings for 700,000 miles.

At the outset Michelin identifies performing learners, not just knowers. Continually, a *cadre* are exchanged to Clermont-Ferrand or Greenville. They do a rigorous stage of teaching, "industrial tourism," and connection to peers from far and wide.

They graft into domains outside of specialty—HR might go into materials, fabrication to finance, and so on. They see to execution of an assignment significant in scope, cross-functional, core to system goals.

This weaves a web of orthogonal thinking, skill grafting, and cultural, professional, and personal ties that bind persons and initiatives in unrehearsed connection. They come to rely on a virtuous form of "cultural appropriation," to transcend their specialty and achieve on the enterprise level.

This web develops and serves, for decades on. Twenty years since *formation*, and this Hoosier still takes calls on bonds Michelin joined from Thailand to Montreal to Ardmore and Cholet.

Question for the reader: How might you render this kind of intentional HR recombinance scheme, simple and visual, on a scale so wide as your enterprise? We will be hearing more on this in the closing chapters.

Restoring *Value Stream Mapping to Intended Use*

Value Stream Mapping (VSM) is popular with OpEx advocates, but has fallen into some disrepute among our coworkers. As practiced, recipients don't always perceive a payoff. Multi-week team investigations are not cheap. What has it told that they didn't already know?

We would do well to restore VSM to its intent, because rightly done it assesses complex systems in a way no other method offers. *Ad fontes*—let's go back to the sources.

Start by asking what is a VSM and the specific benefits it delivers. Nine times out of 10 the proponent's reply is vague. Often it gets called a kind of "flowchart" of what we do. When we talk a lot but don't say much, we cause the organization to miss what VSM is. If we are so unclear on what it is, the hearers are right to feel unsure about deliverables.

It is lean theater, to swap flowcharting symbols for "lean" ones as if that somehow enlightens a plain diagram of sequential chain tasks. VSM is a poor way to try to show tactics like nested conditional decision loops. Fault trees and flowcharts are far better suited to that sort of point analysis. No wonder there is disenchantment with the "Maps" we bandy about.

VSM is no flowchart. It is unsuited to mapping conditionals because its intent isn't the *analysis* of tactics. Its use is in the *synthesis* of system strategy. Practitioners ought to grasp the difference and choose the right tool for the job they are undertaking.

On the phenomenon of *emergence*, favorable arrangements join parts into a system of more abstract capabilities than its subunits. *How we connect within and between layers is what extends systems to new levels of emergent use and order.* This turns out to be the crux of sustaining.

VSM is an instructive way to see the state of system-think. It is uniquely suited to symbolize the manner of complex system *connections*, rendering strategic issues intuitive to any sociological group affected, across the entire span of an extended order. No flowchart can do this.

Unit processes and data boxes are mere incidentals on a VSM, just the means to get at the real question: Does our manner of connection endow the system with abstract, strategic properties like safety, quality, delivery, profit, citizenship? Where does our system fall short of strategic expectation? Who are the affected, and what is the economic loss/opportunity at the enterprise level? What should "improvement" look like over the next 1 to 5 years? Visuality on these kinds of issues is the province of VSM.

CHAPTER 4

Collaboration's Arsenal

Catallaxy—from Greek—literally to change from an enemy into a friend; to voluntarily set up exchange between us, admit the other into community.

Parallels for Enterprise Improvement

Hayek related with simplicity, how *deep structures* work to spawn order at interfaces where the actors mutually extend. He put the principles so clear that GM issued his *Road to Serfdom* to every employee. *Reader's Digest* sent a condensed version to the homes of middle America. Hayek was an economist, but civilization is civilization, and order is order. Parallels stare us right in the face.

Relating Hayek's work on *catallaxy* into operations means translating economic arguments. It is not far from econ to politics. We will stick to our own knitting—sustainment in enterprise.

Artificial intelligence, data routing, and asymmetric warfare are analogs of market *catallaxy*. We find it in language formation,[1] and in pan-African emergence of humanity.[2] It is seen in the tracks of *dense heterarchy*, which put Russian land-bridges in need of reconciliation to oceanic settlement by Vikings and Islanders, if we are to say how the Americas came to be populated. The applicability extends far beyond the assembly of Japanese sedans.

Animals aren't politically conflicted on what works. Nature cracks complexity, on remarkably efficient symbolic information exchanges. If we understand what makes emergence tick, we can better recognize the forces that work to its undoing, when we get to Part II.

It is useful to borrow from nature's tricks. *Self-organization in Biological Systems* is a nice catalogue of object lessons in emergence. Let's start down this trail of lateral thought, with the authors' definition:

> Emergence refers to a process by which a system of interacting subunits acquires qualitatively new properties that cannot be understood as the simple addition of their individual contributions.[3]

Emergence in Chemistry

Sodium (Na) and Chlorine (Cl) are reactive and hazardous. Bonding these poisons yields table salt NaCl, an essential to human health. Hydrogen (H) and Oxygen (O) are combustible gases. They mix but remain combustible gas. But joined in presence of a catalyst, they bond into a nonflammable liquid we call water, H_2O.

Atoms don't pass information the way we think about speech or writing: It is embedded—implicitly—as directional shapes and forces of the constituents themselves. Properties are down payments on modes of connection by which items can self-assemble in their future circumstances. Beneficial attractors are rendered preferential in terms of system energy.

Complex protein structures self-assemble. Tools and furniture are made to copy the same trick. With creativity on form of dunnage, this is exactly how we use visual pull and 5S to perfectly supply complex assembly operations without computers or planners.

Written in the Sand

Dunes are wonders of fractal structure. No human could do so vast an intricacy. The artists of the dunes are gravity, wind, and a property of granules—*critical angle of repose*.

Grains blow into piles. Gravity pulls top ones downward. They sit in equilibrium. A pile grows whose walls tilt further out of horizontal as height increases. Tilt redirects a component of gravity to pull across grains, not just in column with ones underneath. At some height, the wall surpasses a critical angle. Top of the pile slumps down the side, resettling into a more stable cone of gentler angle and wider base. It starts over. The undulating order deposits in its wake a visual recording of the pile's dance across the desert floor.

How grains interact is built into the matter itself. Movements conform to a definite pattern which was no conscious design. We see the same in snowflakes (crystal formation, avalanche, etc.).

Parallels of *self-organized criticality* in manufacturing include accumulators, and flex of cross-trained operators to standard work toggles, in variable-demand flow lines.

Life

Like lifeless materials, plants and microbes employ the **predisposition of shapes and forces**, to promote order extension. In addition, they **transmit genetic code**. Adding code to the cell's playbook makes its kind of order formation **adaptive**. For example, pharmacology struggles to keep pace with MRSA and STDs, which continually advance their resistance to treatment.

Meantime, water is still built the same as it was before Pharaoh swam the Nile. Ability to pass code from one generation to the next kicks the door open to novel formations. Life is more complex than chemicals.

Higher Life

Higher animals too use predisposition of shape and force. They too pass instruction code, to adaptive advantage. To yet further advantage, they have brains with which to plan and think.

Then people have vast cognitive advantage over animals. Tom Wolfe did a fascinating exposition of this in *The Kingdom of Speech*. Our toolbox for order formation is very large.

We adapt devices that can **store** and **transmit** learning: inter-*personally*, inter-*spatially*, and inter-*temporally*. That is our blessing, but also our curse—we tend to overcomplicate. We are too readily convinced that it is smart to stray from mutuality.

Transmitting Information by Exchange of Cues and Signals[4]

The emerging structure itself can be made to serve as rich guidance to the actors. Information deposit into work-in-process (WIP), or workplace, is *stigmergy*. *Stigmergy's* cues and signals are stimuli embedded into workplace or workpiece. Such tapestries are not just decoration.

Indirect Exchange

Cues are laid to inform *incidentally*. Sender and receiver can be separated in space and time. Trails, rutting, scratching, and chemical marking are cues. Price is a cue that enables exchange of valuables inter-temporally and inter-spatially. Spies famously tag posts, ads, and dead drops to exchange secrets. 5S, *kanban*, mailbox flags, *heijunka*, and EVOP sputniks are visual cueing systems.

What governs here? What authority issues orders, foresees future, elaborates plans, and preserves equilibrium? The marvel is how thousands of termites can coordinate their activities to build a mound thousands of times larger than a single individual.

No termite possesses knowledge of the ultimate form of the structure, much less an overview as it takes shape. The building spans several termite lifetimes, making it all the more stunning how it can progress adaptively but unswervingly over time.[5]

By depositing pheromones on the trails the termite walks, and in the balls it rolls, others are stimulated to move or remove pellets of earth and excrement. On an elementary rule-set, simple insects raise pillars, which set others into the generation of fractal order, to a whole so complex that nothing less than an architect could conceive it.

Direct Exchange

Signals are *direct* exchanges of information. Examples include song, gesture, and passing of objects and documents.

Active signals are less open to ambiguity or decay than are passive cues. This comes at a tradeoff: Signals hold the actors in wait for synch. They miss out on opportunity to go cover an extended span of contribution where they don't or can't leave the information to exchange itself opportunistically.

Schooling Fish

The individuals do not need to know a leader, purpose, or destination for remarkable order to form up. They coordinate on physical position of their immediate neighbors.

It is inconceivable that one supervisory individual could monitor every one's position and broadcast the moment-by-moment instructions needed to maintain the school's spatial structure, or that the individual fish could monitor such a directive.[6]

An individual need only hold distance from neighbors, in tolerance. For schooling to emerge, each fish only needs a *kata* for when a gap closes too near, and a *kata* for when a gap opens too far in any direction. Whenever all gaps are in tolerance, just drive on. A rule-set could be made more complex for further orders of schooling. But even this simple one could produce amazing patterns against the variability undersea.

Many nesting patterns take novel, fractal orders of shape on boundary encounters with neighbors. Lightning bugs use flash of immediate neighbors, and a couple of rules, to join and flash their own ends into the global synch.

In Presence of Variability, Information Means Feedback Loop

Our challenge is to sift guidance out of distraction, signal from noise. Data are just observations. Data are plentiful, but *data only answer the question that gets asked or supposed.*

Data are not necessarily information. But information is data (a very specific subset). As Juran put it, *information* is *data that goes to the actual questions we have.*[7]

Communication is no one-way send. It requires receipt, storage, orientation on the joined information, feedback how the try worked, over the span of the affected parties. This runs not in a line, but rather, in a recursive loop.

Feedback can run in a **positive** loop (reward). Where closeness to others means synergy and protection, it is a positive sort of feedback. It can also run in a **negative** loop (recoil from loss). Where collision is at issue, closure to neighbors is a negative form of feedback.

We see complementary pairing of negative and positive feedback, to avoid runaway. Bees close ranks to vibrate in formation, to bring a cooling hive temperature back to setpoint. The same bees alter movement to adjust air convection, if the hive trends too hot.

Alternative Organizations of Actors: Toward Order

One can order a system by imposing external force to shape its arrangement and members' interactions. This way of control is *cognitive*. MRP unit process scheduling is an example. Or, it could be ordered by using the interplay of members as the force that arranges. This way is called *reflexive control*. Replenishment pull is an example of it, in scheduling.

Five Ways of Cognitive Control[8]

Cognitive control can be imposed by directors, prints, recipes, templates, and audits.

Directors

Since the dawn of time autocrats have built organizations void of interaction among the actors in the system. Perhaps the oldest known plant designs are the models from the tomb of Meketre (1985 B.C.), from the Pharaohs' Valley of the Kings. There are models of a brewery, granary, slaughterhouse, and other operations. Consider the organization of the linen mill:

> The linen mill has 11 slaves and a boss. He is the "sensor," the strict arbiter of "Is" versus "Ought". He orders output to his plan by inflicting unpleasant correctives. As Juran pointed out, this sensor creates **action but no information**, an abuse of humanity. As things run, the leader detects change, calculates adjustment needed by each member, and revises orders.

The coxswain is a director who decides overall speed and destination for a rowboat and orders the individual exertions onto his intent. Rowing can be organized as a hybrid: Self-organization among rowers may adjust to their neighbors for micro-coordination, within a coxswain's calls for macro-direction.

Prints

> A blueprint is a compact representation of the spatial or temporal relationships of the parts of a pattern.[9]

Composers pen musical scores. Playwrights do scripts. Choreographers arrange moves in a sequence. Architects lay plans and elevations that they have purposed and conceived. Still, they hire supervisors to adapt individual work to unforeseen variables affecting the execution of the scheme. Design-build architecture is an example of pattern-building using a combination of blueprints and directors, to lay order.

Recipes

sequential instructions that precisely specify the spatial and temporal actions of the individual's contribution to the whole pattern. This lack of adjustment of the building process through feedback from the work in progress epitomizes our definition of a recipe.[10]

Blueprints spell out what to build, not how. Recipes prescribe how—sequence, work content, duration, materials, means used, by whom. Standard conditions and standard work are examples of recipe.

Kalte Rabarbersuppe mit Mokkaeis — Ein richtig schönes Dessert für heiße Sommertage!

Adaptability is a weakness of recipes as an ordering principle. The chef bottlenecks the staff. This setup is inflexible to redirect, replace, or reinforcing the actors mid-step with additional helpers.

Templates

A template is an exemplar that prescribes literally the final pattern a director asks workers to replicate. It spells out what, but not how. It is less abstract than print or recipe, because it is at scale, in 3-D. Little is left to imagine.

In J.L. Borges' tale *On Exactitude in Science*, a cartographers' guild decided to create a greatest-ever map that captured every possible detail about an empire. To contain all that, it ended up point-by-point a copy as big as the empire itself. This ultimate map was too big to store, too unwieldy for spot issues. It was easier for users to go back to trial-and-erroring their way around the real world. They lacked a template that anyone could efficiently and intuitively relate key information.

We only reach higher levels of order through use of abstraction, such as symbols on a map. Not just any old abstraction will do, if the actors are to work reflexively: Our abstract representations need to be intuitive, effective, and information-dense.

We find this in operations that rely on templates to verify quality. To guide a complexity requires a lot of information. Templates that can display that much tend to be space-eaters, inflexible to redirection, replacement.

Template use does not lend well to insertion of help mid-cycle. Interruption requires users to painstakingly relate where things have progressed to, relative to overall structure, and devise a path to resume and divide up the work. Templates create challenges in change-point control and obsolescence. They do relieve abstraction from frontline workers, but lag out of phase with evolving standards and variability in product mix, unless very strict maintenance and rigor is upheld.

Audits

Leaders fall into two camps: managers of ends, or by means.

Ends-auditing (after-the-fact KPI review, with formal Corrective Action Request [CAR]) is among the most common of the cognitive approaches to managing. An attractive alternative is in-process *management by means* to the ends, *hoshin kanri*.

Management of ends is the idea that animates the Project Management movement. If strong leaders can just be insistent enough, and bird-dog enough subordinate details, results get driven. Create a "burning platform." Or so it goes in some circles.

Reductionism deconstructs great problems down into subordinate matrices of objectives, which get driven down through organizational layers. Planners deploy their ends, with elaborate prescriptions on timelines and action registers. Audit drives frequent checking on the fulfillment of intermediate objectives.

Focus shifts to compliance on deadlines, budgets, and milestones, not cause, not learning. Eyes are on outcome, not barriers and resourcing. Discovery along the way is hard to absorb into next steps because "next" is programmed. Mid-course adjustment would complicate deadline discussions (thus, performance appraisals).

Real-world challenges are dynamic, not static. The scientific method—*falsification*—is the unrelenting exposure and overcoming of hidden conditionals. The set-piece battle plans of traditional Project Management are ill-suited for depicting and absorbing hidden conditionals.

Reductionism is simplistic. Juran posited that 20 percent of issues are operator-controllable, 80 percent management-controllable. Doers lack the means to bring output in line with expectation of their directors. Deming argued that management-controllable is closer to 94 percent.

Sproul reminds us—ideas have consequences. Project reductionism drives well-meaning unit leaders to prioritize milestone outcomes over obligations to attend to local means. This is disrespectful, unrealistic, and counterproductive. Eventually, front-liners give up and just go along with the reporting. Compliance, not problem-solving, not producing, wins the day. Henry Ford put this conundrum exactly right:

> If you think of 'standardization' as the best you know today, but which is to be improved tomorrow—you get somewhere.

> But if you think of standards as confining, then progress stops.[11]

Visuality in Auditing: Dashboards

Companies driven by project software, Management Review, and big audit stay captive to the rearview mirror. This lagged game of catch-up can never end.

They gather workers on beautiful dashboards that describe last month's history. A typical dashboard trends things like profitability, units produced per labor hour, utilization percentage, lost time, injury rate, and return on capital employed. Those tasked to do the actual doing, don't have a "profit" knob or "utilization" lever. If they did they would already be wearing it out.

After-the-pipe, enterprise-level metrics are not actionable to doers. Juran called this *gemba* fallacy *information but no action*. It is the mirror image of the leadership fallacy we saw at Meketre, Pharaoh's *action without information*. For directors to come back to mutuality with doers, we must change our thinking (and our boards).

Learn to deploy strategy by managing the throttling of *means*, not just pressurizing wished-for ends. This was alluded to earlier as *hoshin kanri* or strategic alignment. Drivers are better served by the windshield than the rearview mirror. We shouldn't uninstall the mirrors, but mainly we need to keep eyes on the road. Focus on history whose chapters are still being written.

If we want order, not just a lament of the past, we would be better-served to focus our auditing on what value-adders need on the spot, what are their barriers, toward agreed ends. At *gemba*, boards and leaders should serve doers, not the other way around.

- What do I need to know? What do I need to share?
- What are the barriers to achieving what was expected?
- What can I as a servant-leader do to close the gap?

Effective strategy is deployment of means to the ends, not nagging on delinquent KPI.

How Management by Means Beats Management by Objective

In *Factory Physics*[12] Hopp and Spearman make a clear, visual demonstration of how pull outperforms push in production planning. This principle applies in strategy: Reflexive pull for management of means (*hoshin kanri*, concurrent design) convincingly outperforms push MBO and project mentality. *Hoshin* is the implementation of pull in strategy deployment. There are four keys:

Variability   Observability   Efficiency   Robustness

Variability

A great number of things factor into how long it takes to perform an operation.

Cause-and-Effect Diagram:
Causes can be affinitized into 6 great Categories, **6M**:

This visualization is also called a Fishbone or Ishikawa diagram.

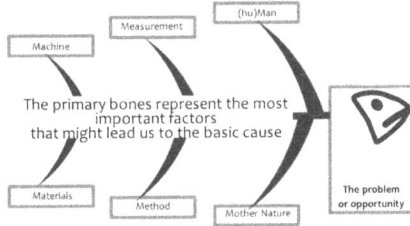

The primary bones represent the most important factors that might lead us to the basic cause

Mother Nature varies, as do hu**M**ans.

Fine instruments reveal that no **M**aterial, **M**ethod, or **M**achine is uniformly repeatable.

Precision reveals that **M**easurements vary.

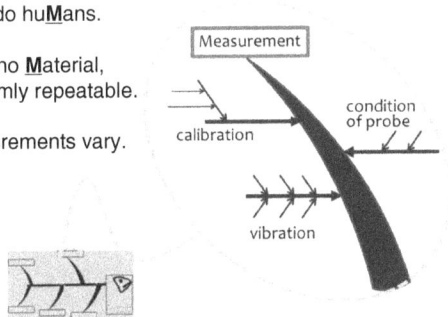

Cycle time to do an action varies. "Normal" is not one singular specified time value:

Time to process falls out on a continuum.

There is always a typical amount of wander, scattered around a central tendency.

No Method is perfectly repeatable. Whether big or small, variation always is.

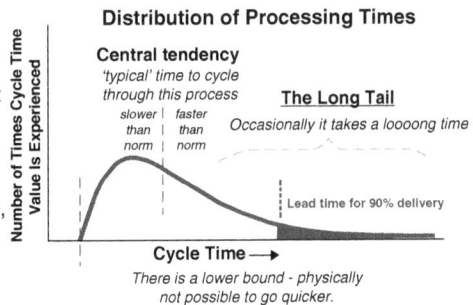

Distribution of Processing Times

Central tendency
'typical' time to cycle through this process

The Long Tail
Occasionally it takes a loooong time

slower | faster
than | than
norm | norm

Lead time for 90% delivery

Cycle Time ⟶

There is a lower bound - physically not possible to go quicker.

Distribution of Processing Times for Push versus Pull Planning

If leadership pushes objectives, WIP independently builds up behind each actor in the system. We can reliably commit to a shorter lead time, across systems managed by pull.

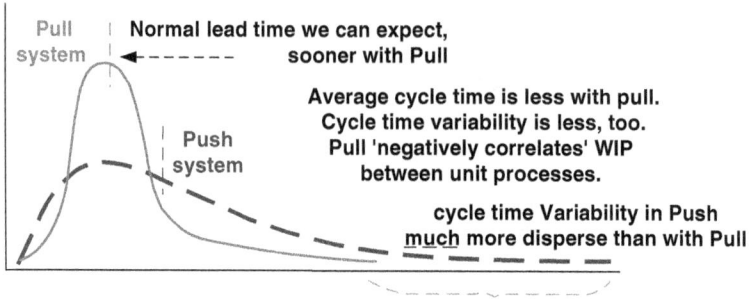

Pull system

Normal lead time we can expect, sooner with Pull

Push system

Average cycle time is less with pull. Cycle time variability is less, too. Pull 'negatively correlates' WIP between unit processes.

cycle time Variability in Push much more disperse than with Pull

Observability

Control is easier if we

- manipulate the stable, easily observed variable (WIP, means) and
- monitor the abstract, sensitive variable (throughput, system KPI) as a resultant.

Control is harder if we

- try to manipulate the sensitive variable (MRP releases, KPI pushes, throughput) and
- monitor the stable, easily observable one (WIP, means) as a resultant.

This is common sense. To see it mathematically, go study PID controller tuning. If we only react **P**roportionally to KPI, outcome will always offset from setpoint. To close the offset requires that we add **I**ntegral and **D**erivative into the scheme. These are esoteric, hard to tune and maintain. Managing to observable means in process, rather than lagged KPI, is a simpler, more reliable way of control over a complex system.

Efficiency and Robustness

Pull is *efficient*—it consumes less resources to execute than push, for any plan chosen. Pull is *robust*: Over a wide range, its profitability is insensitive to planning imperfections.

**Sensitivity of Control and Profit
to Imperfect planning**

If we push past optimum plan, further release of WIP [Overproduction] drives system sharply into financial loss.

In no case does push planning beat profitability of pull.

Push system

Small error in release of WIP into system

Deviation from Perfect Plan

Sharp slope – big impact on profit, loss of <u>control</u>

Profitability — *Loss*

Management of means—*hoshin*—generates pull in strategy deployment.

Leading versus Lagging Indicators, for Control

After-the-pipe KPIs like flow time, profit, and OSHA rate are **lagging** indicators—they yield no feedback on how a system is doing until after a job has exited the system. By then more jobs have balled up at the back and endure the issues that have built up.

Queues and backups are *memoryless*—in the coming days they will not recall how they got there. Traffic jams do not soon drift on their own back to a low-queue state. They require early, forceful intervention. If we flip coins and drift 10 heads above breakeven, we have probability of only 1/1,000 of 10 tails in a row and getting back out of the hole. Randomness is great at creating backups, but things don't right themselves, in any reasonable amount of time.

Control

< Feedback <

Input   effector

Process   Output   Results   detector   Users on the spot

Lagging Indicator
Respond after the fact;
Recover and Resume

Ability to control degrades exponentially with time and distance between the Detector and the Effector

<Feedback<

Input   effector   detector
Process   Output   Results

Real-time indicator
In-process Control
Respond to emerging issues
Product remains salable

Ability to manage outcome improves drastically as we decrease lag time and distance between the detector and the effector. Status of queue in front of a key activity provides a **leading** indicator. We don't have to wait for jobs to exit the system, for feedback that things slowed down or went amiss. Use visuality to render the in-process queue self-announcing. Leaders can respond early and forcefully with resourcing and barrier removal. This is the kind of audit that achieves actual control. It improves exponentially over traditional management of end-audits and formal CARs.

Now we have examined **five ways to cognitive control**, five variants of *hierarchy*. It beats *anarchy*, but the extent of order it can offer is capped by its need for a director who possesses always fresh, thorough grasp of the desired end-state, ability to maintain constant overview of detailed current state everywhere in the system, and to instantly coordinate the on-the-spot adjustments of all the actors.

Hayek, Mises, Pareto, and others showed the mathematical futility of this kind of cognition in the planner, and the actors, once our span reaches much further than a tribe.

In contrast to **cognitive** control, let's take a hard look at the advantages of a **reflexive** approach.

Reflexive Control Approaches

Reflexive offers two basic variants—*stigmergy* and *heterarchy*. Each has its drawbacks. Both are considerably more efficient than cognitive *hierarchy*.

Stigmergy

Stigmergy's actors have only **indirect social interactions**.[13] Information needed by the actors to extend order is embedded into the workplace. Work per the deposited signals is individualistic. Agents at the site neither supervise nor coordinate directly among themselves. This exploits the nimbleness of individualism. Extensive order can be achieved cheaply by workers of minimal cognitive ability. The expense and lag of a boss is unneeded.

Stigmergy is the most tactically efficient (cheapest) way there is to do a plan. But because there are no direct social interactions, the system does not learn and adapt. It explains how termite mounds get built but does not seem to explain when and how the construction should terminate. It is a tactic, not a purpose with a strategy. *Stigmergy* is great as far as it goes, but for us to find sustainment, there will have to be more.

Heterarchy

Hierarchy is **directive arrangement** for purpose deployment.

Aims push down through nested layers, from directors to doers. Feedback backup toward directors is incidental and mostly subsequent to formation of strategy. Peer interaction is incidental, more like communication than co-adaptation of the plan.

Heterarchy is a **feedback arrangement** for purpose deployment.

The actors adaptively flex among various roles, contextually. Transmission is primarily peer to peer. Vertical communication with direction flows two ways.[14] The U.S. Marines are an excellent example. A firm operating to *Takt* attainment is the best business example.[15]

Heterarchy balances elements of central purpose and direction with the bulk of control distributed to tactical levels. It is characterized by adaptiveness of roles, to continually re-tune for effectiveness of feedback, not one-way directives. Specialization enables groups to extend order beyond individualism, by recombining members on mutuality. The actors fine-tune the plan by collaboration. Advancement is efficient, mostly through direct interaction of peers.

While a *heterarchy* is hunting, the tracker may be the one who directs, generally arranging the members and zones. Later when they migrate, a guide may step up, and the tracker reverts to former role. Once migrated, a builder may take the lead. *Heterarchy* organizes adaptive, contextual combinations that blend an element of overall direction, with tactical coordination decentralized and worked out peer to peer.

First-Order Benefits of Co-adaptation

On the surface, there is direct and immediate boost to one or both parties, just from associating. Peter Corning catalogs several first-order benefits[16]:

Complementary Functions

One half cup of beans provides the nutritional equivalent of two ounces of steak.

Three cups of whole wheat flour provides the equivalent of five ounces of steak.

Eaten separately, they amount to seven ounces of steak . . . . consumed together they provide the equivalent of 9.3 ounces of steak, or 33% more usable protein.[17]

Augmentation and Facilitation

Catalysts decrease threshold for other things to react, but catalyst goes unchanged.

Environmental Conditioning

Penguins huddle to reduce energy expenditure by 50 percent.

Risk and Cost Sharing

Flocking, collective foraging, carpools, and insurance are common examples.

Higher-Order Benefits of Co-adaptation

Beneath the surface, great interaction effects emerge from mutual association. These can be lumped under the heading of **Comparative Advantage**.

Consider an illustration from emergency medicine:

> Bob and Sue are doctors. They respect one another and set up shared practice. It involves two aspects. Workload is about even—one person's worth of each:
> - Emergency surgery (which is value-adding),
> - Value-aiding administration (triage, patient prep, cleaning, restocking, etc.).
>
> Surgery is the why the firm exists. It gets the applause, but can't do without admin.
>
> Admin is means to an end. It is subordinated to surgery. But it can't be devalued if this association is to succeed. One of the doctors is going to have to do it. Consider the two partners' productivity:

	Sue	Bob
Emergency surgery	4/hour	3/hour
Admin	5/hour	4/hour

Sue has *absolute advantage* in every area. She is faster than Bob in surgery. She is faster also in admin. She is just plain fast. This is not to say she should do all. It does not diminish Bob's importance, for us to state facts. He serves a vital role:

Comparative Advantage = who can act at lowest *enterprise-level* cost.

Who has higher *output* is kind of a distraction here. We cannot afford to overlook what is best for the whole, to the glory of a subunit. Comparative advantage is system-thinking. To do less sells the partners short, which tends to rivalry and hard feelings, the opposite of mutuality.

To Wisely Delegate

To delegate is to trade off. Choosing one means choosing not to do its alternatives. To have this, we will not have that other. To properly delegate, we don't compare absolute advantages—we must compare opportunity cost.

Opportunity Cost = the opportunity we pass up, to do this

Opportunity cost in our surgery example:

If Sue does the admin (5/hour), Bob will only complete surgery on 3.
If instead Bob does the admin (4/hour), Sue can do surgery on all 4.
Opportunity cost of having Sue do admin is 1 less life saved, per hour. Bob needs to serve them and community, by keeping Sue at the scalpel. She and community should honor Bob: His value-aid makes Sue's prodigious value-adding possible.

Voilà, the magic of comparative advantage. Partners specialize to exploit that the other is in the mix. Coadaptation has made some of their former exertions redundant.

Symbiotic Hunting Pairs: Advantage at Several Levels

Badgers and coyotes form hunting pairs. These predators do not share one aim. They don't like each other—they don't have to. Badgers are good at digging up prey. Coyotes are better at lookout and are nimble enough to run down prey that evades badgers.

Consider a badger who splits time evenly between digging and lookout. Take his neighbor coyote who spends 30 percent of time digging prey, 50 percent running it down, and 20 percent on lookout. When the two join, the magic of specialization unfolds on three levels[18]:

    I. Spatial Association.

       Because both are present, both can reduce the fraction of time they spend on lookout.

       No rearrangement of other duties is involved, initially. Both just get by with less lookout, which leaves more time for the normal mix of other duties.

    II. One partner remixes its behavior.

       Badger uses freed-up lookout time to dig more, now 80 percent of time, and 20 percent lookout (no longer half and half). Both he and Coyote get more to eat, even if Mr. Coyote doesn't change his mix. It isn't a model of "fairness" but both are better off.

   III. Both parties mutually specialize and change behavior.

   IV. If Mr. Coyote quits digging and instead devotes 70 percent to chasing and 30 percent on lookout, the badger gets better warning because the coyote's long-distance surveillance is better than his. Badger just digs and eats. Coyote looks out and eats. Both partners gain, not just incidentally but through co-adapted specialization.

Improvement is the science of information. Some gain comes of deductive reasoning. But life is so complex—most of what we learn to advance our aims is what we sift out of experience. Relentless induction of science can accelerate the sifting, to identify patterns that favor beneficial order. It is good at outing hidden conditionals, to then take advantage. These are approaches of the mind—study—of problems. We face more problems than we can study. The academic bent taken by the developed countries since the early 1900s has caused us to rate-limit improvement to the capacity of experts. We mostly leave frontline workers out of the game. Nature serves a wake-up call.

The very shape of workplace and workpiece can be exploited to favor self-assembly of order. Forces within the materials can likewise be exploited. Passing code makes improvement not just efficient but adaptive. We can do it on signals or cues. Cells and the lowliest animals model great cleverness in how. Anyone can do this.

Our *kingdom of speech*—reporting, data collecting, boards, and other devices—can transmit learning inter-personally, inter-spatially, inter-temporally, in ways animals can't conceive.

We overcomplicate and are too easily swayed that it is smart to stray from mutuality. Nature reminds us of the great arsenal of weapons at our disposal, besides deductive and inductive studies. Not just elites, but everyone, everywhere, every day can solve problems.

Hopefully the examples of this chapter can help restore this kind of mutuality in our enterprises.

CHAPTER 5

Breakthrough

Even a trade, the pride and security of every worker, no longer lasts a lifetime. Our largest single labor union is the Teamsters. How many of their members still drive a team of horses?[1]

—J.M. Juran

Paradigm—from the Greek paradeigma—the ability to see resemblances between apparently disparate problems.[2]

—Thomas Kuhn

This chapter spotlights key sources Thomas Kuhn and J.M. Juran, on the nature of breakthrough. Seeing how it forms up sheds light on behaviors and reactions that beset and undo it.

In *Managerial Breakthrough*, Juran notes how 98 percent of species that have shared earth are now extinct. Entropy is a bear. Products, services, and ways are mortal.[3] Some orders are good. But none is permanent. Heraclitus put it, *you can't step into the same river twice.* Today's order may extend, or unravel, but it will change. To transcend a current order, we must guard an adaptive strategy that promotes the emergence of mutuality at equal-to-or-greater-than replacement rate.

Kuhn's *Structure of Scientific Revolutions* was one of the most influential works of the 20th century. Like Juran, Kuhn isolated the **universal breakthrough sequence** and reactions it brings. He offers us great advice on how to go forward more peaceably than is the norm.

Starting Point

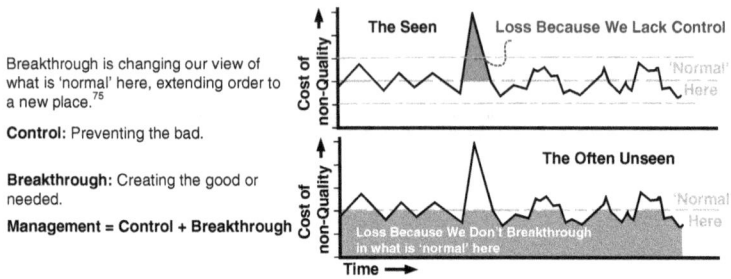

The Seen

Loss Because We Lack Control

Breakthrough is changing our view of
what is 'normal' here, extending order to
a new place.[75]

'Normal'
Here

Control: Preventing the bad.

The Often Unseen

Breakthrough: Creating the good or
needed.

'Normal'
Here

Management = Control + Breakthrough

Loss Because We Don't Breakthrough
in what is 'normal' here

Time →

Challenge the standard as much as the variance.[5]

Breakthrough and control come when we act like learners—neither complacent victors nor surrendered victims. Often breakthrough arises in extremity of need, or when optimists go all in on an opportunity. Either way, breakthrough's starting point is *epistemic humility.*

Motivated learners inductively try their way to success, refusing to be denied. Wins start piling up, confidence swells—a critical mass starts seeing issues as opportunities. They march forth and subdue. They conjecture and try, in forward-running loops. They discover technologies and cures. They ride these to surges of progress and peace. From this pinnacle, they take on an expectancy of unbroken progress. Why ever not?

But reality sets in—discovery isn't linear. Progress does not run in an inevitable, utopian arc. There are plateaus and reversals. Improvement initiatives fail to sustain. Our relationship with change is complicated. Advancement brings us to face our nature. To mitigate self-defeating pauses takes system thinking—ideas have consequences.

The Structure of Scientific Revolutions

In this great source, Kuhn laid out the universal breakthrough sequence, in five stages:

1 Conception—Experimentation

First focus – find technologies and cures. Learners exploit findings and de-mystify their status quo.

The Scientific Method is the most effective device known, for penetrating the threshold of this kind of knowledge, traversing challenges and unknowns.

Induction is very good at this stuff.

1 Normal Science

2 Application

Things settle in for a time of great, but mostly methodological discovery.

This phase majors on the application and exploitation of the base discoveries.

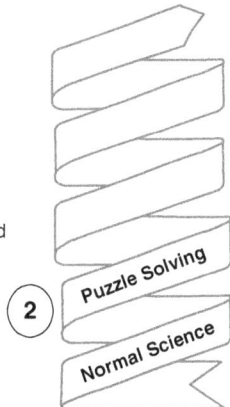

2 Puzzle Solving

Normal Science

3 Mental Models—Scaffolding—Extend the Paradigm

Core assumptions on cause and effect get solidified, open questions mostly resolved. Explanatory power on issues up to now has been great.

- New paradigms on cause and effect become kind of a social given. Taking for granted gives velocity in puzzle-solving the next questions about the issues we face.

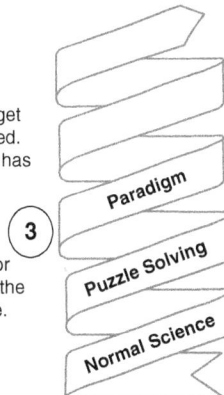

3 Paradigm

Puzzle Solving

Normal Science

4 Overreach: Gaps Exposed in Explanatory Power of the Paradigm

Starting from a prevailing paradigm speeds up next inquiries. We eventually presume into domains where it lacks explanatory power.

Mainstream paradigms experience embarrassing gaps. Rival explanations are needed to explain the gaps.

→ dissent grows

  → institutional pushback on 'deniers'

    → recourse to philosophy

      → forced to revisit base assumptions

'Your arms are too short to box with math.'

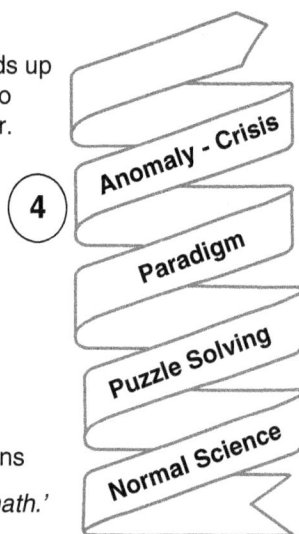

5 Revolution

"Out of this new ferment new ideas arise, new methods, and finally a new theory."

—Ian Hacking

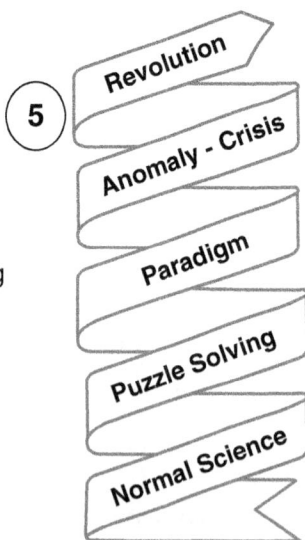

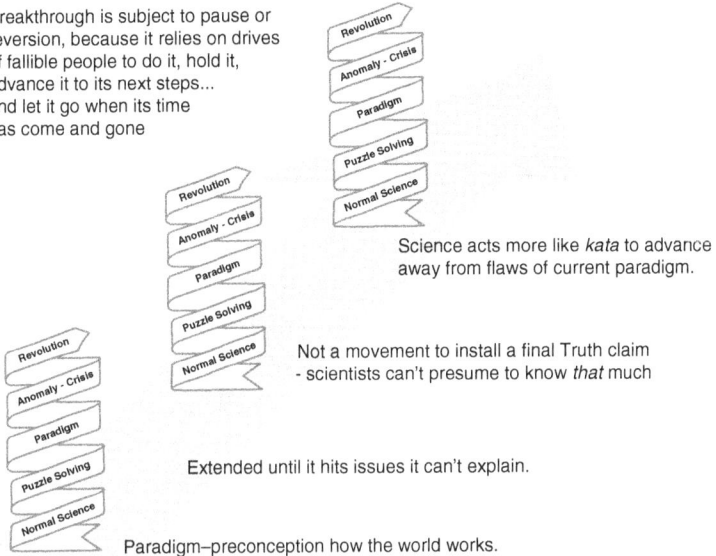

Breakthrough is subject to pause or reversion, because it relies on drives of fallible people to do it, hold it, advance it to its next steps... and let it go when its time has come and gone

Science acts more like *kata* to advance away from flaws of current paradigm.

Not a movement to install a final Truth claim - scientists can't presume to know *that* much

Extended until it hits issues it can't explain.

Paradigm–preconception how the world works.

Incommensurability of Deeply Held Worldview

We will see in Part II, *incommensurability*[7] is a key failure mode in the breakthrough cycle. This defect in how we intersect is key to when success quits extending into sustainment.

Every paradigm gets projected further into new domains, until eventually it overreaches. As well as it has served, eventually it runs up against things it is not good at explaining. If something is important and demands proper explaining, failure of establishment paradigms to do so leads to crisis among leaders.

On the surface of it, all the parties superficially use the same vocabulary words to debate the issue. But there are profound limitations to what proponents of opposing worldviews can manage to even transmit to one another (let alone agree on). They use the same word to express two irreconcilable things. They hear but they do not perceive what the other says. The partisans cannot, will not.

For all our pretense of tolerance and progress, behavior when confronted with new (read: rival) paradigms presents socially more like boorish reaction to faith conversion, than a considerate inquiry.

Constructive advice[8] on how to handle *incommensurability* may be Kuhn's key contribution on resistance and backsliding. We will revisit this in Part III, in which we propose countermeasures to help us sustain and advance.

Juran: A Universal Breakthrough Sequence

Juran spent his 104-years up-fitting government and industry for breakthrough. He authored the *Quality Handbook*, a collection of primers on methods. His other works are perhaps an even greater legacy. Learners built storied *Production Systems* upon them in 1950s–1970s Japan. Juran left to each category of "us" in enterprise a how-to guide for breakthrough and sustaining:

In *The Corporate Director* Juran mentors the role and work of an effective board.

His works on the *Quality Planning process* like *The Quality Trilogy*[9] reset the paradigm of engineering and management—quality can't be inspected in. For quality to be realistic means to design it in at conception of product and process. Juran laid out the behavioral roadmap.

Bureaucracy kindly mentors[10] those who **referee alternative use of intramural resources** (goods whose relation is not allocated by market price[11]) on how to sustain bearings and heading. All complex enterprise entails a surprising amount of this kind of coordination. Leaders bristle if called *bureaucrats*, but internal tradeoff is part of extended order. Every coordinator is a bureau: As Sproul put it, any choice I get is not whether I will be one, but rather, *Will I be a good or a bad one?* Bureaucratic reality, good or ill, is highly consequential to the prospects for efficiency and especially to *Holding the Gains*. In this brief 1944 allegory, Juran laid out behaviors that people now like to call 5S, flow versus batch-and-queue, Eight Wastes, Value Stream Mapping, *jidoka*, *poka yoke*, and so on.

Quality Improvement Tools (early 1980s) may still be the finest workbooks for equipping front line operators. They mentor simple, visual tools *any* member can do, with test cases to self-discover appropriateness, fallacies, and misuses. These are great equalizers of members, antidotes to caste-signaling with "belts" and big math. Sustainment means all hands on deck. Of the great sources, especially Juran equips operators to contribute in strategy.

Managerial Breakthrough is Juran's workday guidebook for **enterprise managers**.

Einstein supposedly remarked that *perfection of means and confusion of goals characterize our age*, and *Theories should be as simple as possible, no simpler*.

Juran too was notably concerned that the way leaders train, resource, and promote "tools" constitutes a serious impediment to breakthrough and sustaining.

Programs to take improvement enterprise-wide often distort the means into ends and conflate "simple" with simplistic distortion. Juran restores context-appropriateness, and recognition of common fallacies, and pitfalls. He undoes *scientism* and rote tool-pushing. He highlighted the role of interactions as the central cause in complexity. His works on unintended consequence, and resilience when falsified, are distinctive among the well-known voices in quality and management.

What Is Breakthrough?

Juran's view of breakthrough is to achieve *fundamental change in the inherent capability* of a system, a paradigm shift as to what becomes the *new normal* here. Resolving chronic issues requires (1) structured approach, (2) reliance on data, and (3) use of appropriate tools, by all persons / levels. Juran painted an indelible picture of what breakthrough looks like:

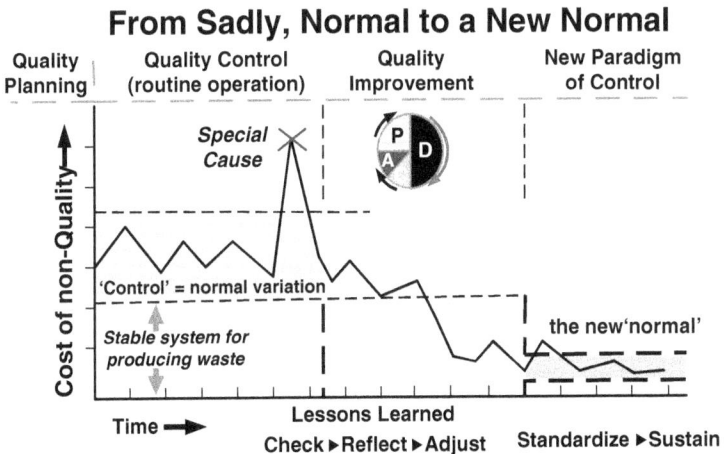

From Sadly, Normal to a New Normal

| Quality Planning | Quality Control (routine operation) | Quality Improvement | New Paradigm of Control |

Special Cause

P A D

Cost of non-Quality →

'Control' = normal variation

Stable system for producing waste

the new 'normal'

Time →

Lessons Learned
Check ▶ Reflect ▶ Adjust   Standardize ▶ Sustain

He distills down to a universal **12-step "Breakthrough Sequence"** in **four phases**[12]:

Phase 1: Project Definition and Organization

First, learners effect **Breakthrough in Attitude** (paradigm), then **Organization**. We know we have arrived when priorities, a valid problem-statement, resources, and metrics align.

Phase 2: Diagnostic Journey

A real doctor diagnoses before presuming to write prescriptions. Diagnosis leads to **Breakthrough in Knowledge**. We can know we have done so when we can verifiably go past the fruit, down to the *root* of an issue.

Phase 3: Remedial Journey

Once cause is isolated, remedy often suggests itself. It confirms that we have gotten this far, when we see **Breakthrough in Cultural Patterns**.

Juran and his peers were indispensable to mobilizing "Rosie the Riveter" out of laundries and kitchens, into resistant industry, revitalizing to win a World War. He cautions experts that *most of a remedial journey* is spent identifying and responsibly handling cultural paradigms. Appetite for (constancy of) purpose in culture change is uncommon in corporate handling of problem-solving.

Adventurers settle cheap for imagined "pragmatism." This is evident in the bruised loyalty and morale of the workplace. Juran encouraged experts to not imagine theirs is a "solution," no matter how technical, which does not entrain **unintended, social consequences**.[13]

- If a problem-solver can't say what was the unintended consequence of their doings, they did the scheme not with, but to, the users.

In a book on not sustaining, by a recovering engineer and plant manager, I confess that this strikes me like a thunderbolt. Once we have followed up our "solution" mutually with the affected, to address the unintended and social consequences, we finally earn the right to call ours a "Remedy."

Phase 4: Hold the Gains

The final phase is **Breakthrough in Results**. We can confirm that we have achieved this phase when we can demonstrate control at the new level.

Concretely how to do so is the topic of Part III of this book. Stay tuned.

Closing Part I

We have examined the mechanics of how self-ordering mutuality can multiply efficiency and the public good. But we should ask:

If emergence is "all that," why doesn't everybody, everywhere do it all the time?

In Part II, we will see the mechanics of resistance and backsliding. Even the most amazing improvements fail to sustain, mostly. There is much about our nature that we need to come to grips with.

This sets the stage for Part III in which we offer countermeasures, toward sustainment.

You don't need much imagination to see that we are building a case for management by means—*hoshin kanri*—in strategic purposing of the enterprise, *Takt* attainment for effective tactical alignment, and broad application of the tools of *stigmergy* to efficiently make the most of our efforts.

Before leaving for Part II, we will take one more historic-civilizational example.

CHAPTER 6

Ad Fontes

To the sources!

—Erasmus

In the rise of Egypt over its first three Dynasties, emergence put on quite a demonstration. By the time Moses confronts Pharaoh (18th–19th Dynasty) synergy is displaced by *scientism*—of the kind we see still undoing sustainment in present-day enterprise. The Fertile Crescent is a classic case where mutual co-adaptation (lean principles) gave way to atavism and abuse of *hierarchy*.

The Nile begins in Uganda. It flows up through a great Sahara Desert. At the coast of Egypt, it empties across a delta of deposited silt, into the Mediterranean. The river pulses on a strong seasonal flood cycle (not unlike demand variability in manufacturing). At even a short distance from the riverbank, during the dry months an unimproved Sahara is a tough place to scratch out a subsistence. Times would be rugged and short. No one is served by bemoaning what others have, or what we don't have. Achievers deeply reflect on what they *do* have, to tease out some potential it might hold toward bettering their circumstances. **Recombinance**, anyone?

To the benefit of millions this happened in Antiquity, on the Nile. Some hunter-gatherer saw past harsh seasonality, that vast alluvial soil deposits hold potential for fine crops. Some other nomad recognized if he could save up enough to not starve through the risk of settling in one place, and levying up a stock of water, he could meter it out to level and radically mitigate the seasonality of soil conditions. They reacted these ideas under catalyst of mutuality, and voilà they got an agricultural, nutritional, learning, and trading explosion. **Level pull**, anyone?

Earthworks alone would set this idea beyond reach of hermits. Consider the inter-temporal patience—from time of initial investment in levying up water, until harvest of predictability and income, deferred years into the future. Passers-by had to submit to delayed gratification, not pillaging precious stock midseason. Specialization and mutuality were needed, for this thing to yield.

The first farmers didn't know it, but they were moral philosophers. Property rights got ironed out and respected—a rule-set that preserved fledgling cooperation trying to find footing. Another "philosopher" realized that by irrigation they could get The Big Idea (water) to carry itself for miles from a riverbank. This interspatial abstraction again amplified specialization, efficiency, variety of crops, and livestock. More neighbors could release the potential of water and silt, on an extended season, over an expanding reach, to grow more than they would eat.

They exchanged surplus for clothing, learning, diversification of herd and seed, transport, expansion of *catallaxy* to "others," up and down the Nile, to Tigris, Euphrates, and beyond. Institutions of interpersonal law in the Third Dynasty (around 2600 B.C.) extended this. Property (thus, invention that improved it) was *"individual and inviolable."* Safe passage got worked out. Collaborators with their rule-sets adapted, and civilization flourished.

These arrangements were giving way by the Fifth Dynasty. For what things were like, see the struggles of Chapter 41 in *Genesis.* By the time Moses arrived on the scene around 1400 B.C., the means and producers had been put under the dominion of slave-abusing autocrats. Ruling whim crushed stirrings of mutual co-adaptation. Edict carried to the minutest details of doers' lives. Command economy prevailed. The world's greatest empire withered.

Hayek cites how other ancients too (the constitution-makers in ancient Crete, the Mycenaeans, and Greeks) extended order through co-adaptation. Classical education and representative republic were born of it. Spartans atavistically resisted mutuality to the point they were said to encourage theft. He relates Cicero's account of Corinth and Carthage rising by mastery of trade and navigation. Rome absorbed these into its own model, to extend the ordering principle to *"all the known world."*

Decline followed on the technocratic pretense that Rome could effectively centralize such a far-flung, elaborate co-adaptation.

Wengrow and Graeber trace Paleolithic trails of *dense heterarchy* through art, trade, clothing, materials, architecture, and large-scale recruitment of labor. They trace emergent achievements from Kraków to Kiev, savannahs of Brazil and Africa, the American plains, from Siberia, to the Don, to the Dordogne. Carole Crumley traces the same trail in Burgundy. David Stark traces it in collaboration of miners in gold rushes of the American West, among other places.

Down the medieval Rhine, industrial, literary, agricultural, educational, linguistic, and healthcare revolutions—*Renaissance*—blossomed out of the coordinating principles of tolerance and inquiry by Erasmus, Agricola, Reuchlin, Gutenberg, and others. Science emerged—not from rigid exercise of dominion, but of loosely collaborative common sense of doers across northern Italy, Switzerland, Alsace, Germany, the Low Countries, pockets in England, and the like.

While the big guys were busy with palace intrigue and murder, *Alsaciens* and *Schwarzwälder* just worked most of it out through the power of mutuality and emergence.

The next sections of this book promote those *deep structures* that already showed us emergence on a continental scale, peaceful inclusion of very different "others," making the best use of those others' fragmentary, dispersed knowledge.

And especially, how to make it stick.

PART 2

Isolate the Forces
of Abandon-and-Revert

Part 2: Isolates the beliefs, arrangements, and counterforces that drive backsliding.

Misconceptions how order arises sow and incentivize its undoing. Collaboration gets reshaped and denatured by our notions of how to achieve "control." Processes and people get reconnected in ways that dis-favor the adaptive pursuit of discovery among peers. Our popular, expert-centric ways of trying to maintain order, undo that which could have promoted its re-extension into further gains.

CHAPTER 7

Unsubscribing from Mutuality and Abstraction

The knowledge of the circumstances of which we must make use never exists in concentrated or integrated form, but solely as the dispersed bits of incomplete and frequently contradictory knowledge which all the separate individuals possess.[1]

—F.A. Hayek

If you live like no one else, later you can live like no one else.
—Dave Ramsey

A Universal Failure Mode

Modern enterprise is extended order, complex. Every failure to sustain has its own reasons. Still, in every case one common disconnect is always implicated: Sustainment un-does when members **unsubscribe from the abstract rule-set**, which had been guiding how we agree to connect. To abandon-and-revert is to **un-share from the mutuality** in which we had joined at our interfaces.

Mutuality and abstract rule-connection are inseparable. Somehow we get persuaded that we could gain order—advantage—going it alone, or sticking to our own kind. We check out. This is backsliding to atavism—raw ambition, or tribalism. It returns to other-izing those who don't share my aims. End-connection displaces abstract-mutual conduct, taking over guidance of how—IF—we will even connect from now on. In justice and governance, this is called coming under *"rule of men,"* rather than "the *rule of law."* The parallels in enterprise sustainment are obvious.

Emergence

We connect our fragmentary knowledge of circumstances using rules of conduct we agree benefit us mutually. Joint, efficient rearrangements form up to surpass any outcome we could have reached, "*everyone for his or herself.*" The whole is better off, often radically so.

There can be localized setbacks, because it is rearrangement after all. Cooperation is still better, even for ones who are countercyclically set back: It is an apex form of adaptation. It is more resilient than we could go off and claw back by raw individualism. If I'm the one who had the setback, this principle may not be easy to see. *Recession is when your neighbor loses his job. Depression is when you are the one who lost the job.*

Conditions for Self-Organizing Extension

Emergence requires connection among participants in **mutuality**. We pursue interests within rules of conduct that apply voluntarily, equally. This prerequisite joins information and efforts as far as members can stretch their mutually agreed web of rules, in wide-ranging, creative pursuit of their several aims.

> Abstract-mutuality nets a greater span of fragmentary information than say, how far a tribe can audit members' conformity and enforce one, prescribed aim.

Mutuality Decline = Decline of Order and Discovery

The runt ancestor of abstract-mutuality is enforced conformity to concrete ends, or else. Interfaces with those who hold differing aims become boundaries of them and us. These could rather have been sites of extension, at least for that on which we do mutually agree. What claim clans can lay to mutuality is the demand that all members agree to the prescribed aims. This limited mutuality puts them ahead of hermits and rangers. But tribalism reaches no further than what they can try in unison. It stays stuck in lower order because it is end-connected.

Inclusiveness—Not Checking Out—Is What Extends Order Formation

The span of persons, viewpoint diversity, and aims of others we join into a rule-set determines the reach of fragmentary information they return to the sum. This determines how far order has the potential to be extended, in any novel rearrangements we can come up with.

We need not know others' aims. We need only agree how participants will (not) acceptably connect. The more complex the undertaking, the greater extent of abstraction it will create (what do we have, and who has claim to it).

Atavism Is Not Better, But It Is Easier, Under Pressure

Mutuality is persuasion that a whole will attain greater than the sum of parts. People under pressure can't eat principles. Abstract-mutuality asks us to submit to rules, through circumstances that don't favor us this time around. A person can't wholly grasp the reasons bound up in rules for a system that extends to persons they will never see. Impatience and hardship in a moment undermine agreement with the unseen "others." It is hard to stick by our word and amend with integrity. It is easy to check out of the deal.

The martyr Jim Elliot said, *He is no fool who gives up what he cannot keep, to gain what he cannot lose.* To pass up a spot advantage to uphold principled rule-connection with rivals, flies in the face of instinct. Abstract order pits immediate gratification against a longer view of reward.

Some check out, sustainment falters, when the value proposition of relief now wins out over the longer-term reward a rule-set stands for. Maintaining *consent of the governed* is a vital, continuous demand of leadership.

CHAPTER 8

Resistance to Improvement

When an ordinary human being strides forward, there are parts of him moving backward. The [corporate] organism is infinitely more sprawling and complicated in its motion.[1]

Few are the places . . . where the gulf of remoteness is broader than in the dealings between an employee and those who make personnel decisions affecting his welfare.[2]

—J.M. Juran

It is useful to recap the deep source work Juran left on the resistance that comes with gain.

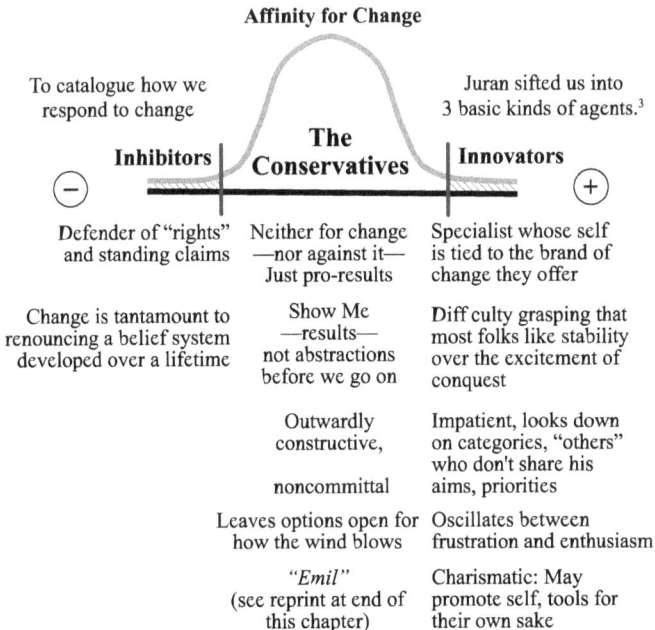

Affinity for Change

To catalogue how we respond to change

Juran sifted us into 3 basic kinds of agents.[3]

Inhibitors $(-)$	The Conservatives	Innovators $(+)$
Defender of "rights" and standing claims	Neither for change —nor against it— Just pro-results	Specialist whose self is tied to the brand of change they offer
Change is tantamount to renouncing a belief system developed over a lifetime	Show Me —results— not abstractions before we go on	Diff culty grasping that most folks like stability over the excitement of conquest
	Outwardly constructive, noncommittal	Impatient, looks down on categories, "others" who don't share his aims, priorities
	Leaves options open for how the wind blows	Oscillates between frustration and enthusiasm
	"Emil" (see reprint at end of this chapter)	Charismatic: May promote self, tools for their own sake

Instinctive Reflex to Change

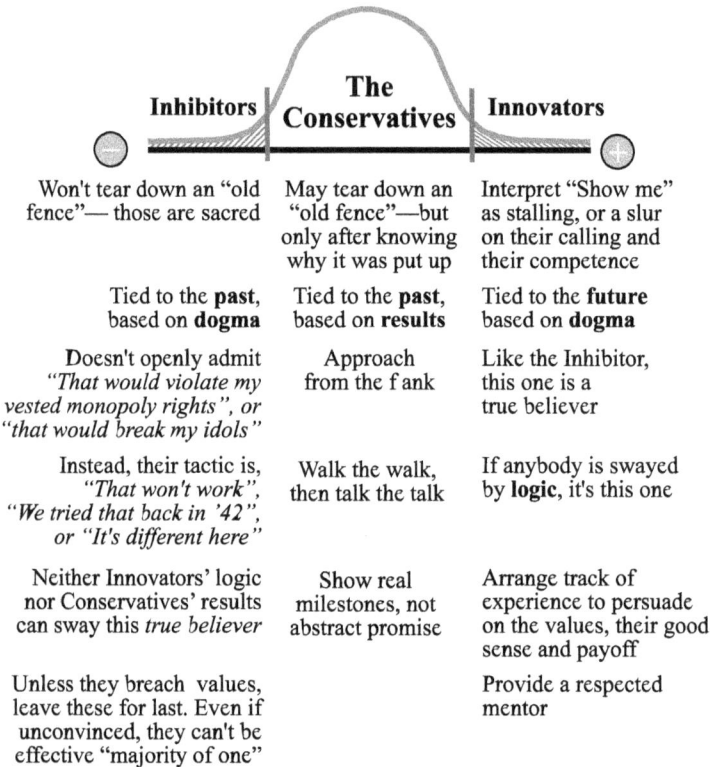

Inhibitors	The Conservatives	Innovators
Won't tear down an "old fence"— those are sacred	May tear down an "old fence"—but only after knowing why it was put up	Interpret "Show me" as stalling, or a slur on their calling and their competence
Tied to the **past**, based on **dogma**	Tied to the **past**, based on **results**	Tied to the **future** based on **dogma**
Doesn't openly admit *"That would violate my vested monopoly rights"*, or *"that would break my idols"*	Approach from the f ank	Like the Inhibitor, this one is a true believer
Instead, their tactic is, *"That won't work"*, *"We tried that back in '42"*, or *"It's different here"*	Walk the walk, then talk the talk	If anybody is swayed by **logic**, it's this one
Neither Innovators' logic nor Conservatives' results can sway this *true believer*	Show real milestones, not abstract promise	Arrange track of experience to persuade on the values, their good sense and payoff
Unless they breach values, leave these for last. Even if unconvinced, they can't be effective "majority of one"		Provide a respected mentor

Getting good at problem-solving means learning to push through, with relentless trying. Setback may take the form of a cause difficult to track back to its lair. Or, for known causes, we may struggle to isolate an appropriate remedy. Opposition of ones invested in the *status quo* is a barrier. Not dismissing, but processing resistance is key to improvement that sustains.

To control means managing a feedback loop, not guiding a stream of one-way directives.

Resistance Is a Signal

Hold on to a little humility. We are not always right. Even when right on the *matter*, we may be unwise on the *manner* we intend to change.

The hesitation experts see as "resistance" is often a tell that the affected have more to say, but won't. Why? Everyone benefits to find the underlying concern and its drivers.

To knowers, the best defense is a good offense—propositional shock and awe. Do we really think that crafting a peerless proposal can substitute for gaining understanding and consent of the affected? When the lights go down and adoring crowds go home, it won't be sales—it will be the users we ask to stick around and make this thing go.

Loyal Opposition

Innovators often seem to tie their image to others' validation of their insight. Disagreeing on the merits veers close to motives, and can go personal in a flash. It is possible to not align with their objections on the merits, yet support their motive for resisting a change. This takes strength and grace. In the heat of trying to persuade, it is easy to lose sight that loyal opposition is a most benevolent thing another could do for us.

Victor Davis Hanson's *Carnage and Culture* recounts nine famous pivots in history where the *kata* of humility and loyal opposition turned civilizations. Colleagues' hesitance may signal their concern that we missed something:

- We may not have recognized certain stakeholders, how affected.
- Our proposal poses risk to future effectiveness.
- We may have missed the actual issue or cause.
- Though right on cause, proposed remedies may not be effective or durable.
- The cure sounds worse than the disease.
- Can we realistically expect to monitor and hold in the future?

We all know insufferable knowers. But can learners afford to dismiss the message, just because we didn't like how it got delivered? There are times to go slow, so we can go fast.

Wisdom, respect, and mutuality are much needed in the agency of change.

Do They Mistake What Consensus Means?

There is a difference between rejecting input and genuinely weighing but not following it. This important distinction is blurred if our expert has a history of railroading "progress" and "the need of the many."

Popular notion has it that "consensus" means to settle on what all can willingly support. It is treated like some vague form of unanimous. "Shared aims" is a fairy tale. Ideas have consequences: this sentimental fallacy ends up pitting "team players" against holdouts, treating them as enemies of the common good.

Consensus looks more like harmony than unison. Artificial striving for unity theatre trades away excellence for a least common denominator. It degrades team dynamic into enforced group-think. Bullying viewpoint-minorities is no prescription for progress. Gwendolyn Galsworth got this one exactly right[4]:

> Consensus is the art of deliberately surfacing where we disagree, so that we can agree which of the rival ideas we will go test.

Let's try a different prescription—one of mutuality, respect, emergent co-adaptation.

Influence Is Best Seen as Earned

Where there is collaborative mutuality, it would be unnatural not to have the adaptive input of the affected. Agents who only pretend to listen ought to forfeit influence in proportion to their pretense. The grant of influence does not mean everyone gets veto rights. None should presume influence beyond how much of our own "stuff" is invested, on the line, in the question at hand.

Their Objection May Be an Indirect One

Modern enterprise is complex, with tradeoffs being resolved in multiple places at the same time. One's objection over here may be indirect— easier to object here than speak up over there where the core issue is un-discussable. Underneath "what" the person is objecting to it is important for the change agent to dig down to "why."

- Connected to people of the old way;
- Loss of status because they derived their status from being good at the old;
- Fear they lack capacity, competence for the change;
- Question the motives of the reformer or the referees; and
- Plain selfish or antisocial.

Dealing with the "Obstructionist" Superintendent[5]

J.M. Juran, *Industrial Quality Control*, July 1955 reprint courtesy of ASQ

". . . a young executive was eagerly relating how they had reduced waste in his company, how through quality control they had discovered some new things about the process, and how the production superintendent had taken action.

One of the listeners shrugged his shoulders. "In my company you wouldn't get to first base with that, and all because of Emil."

Emil, it turned out, was an "old time" production superintendent. Emil was set in his ways. Nothing could make him change. And the management was just too softhearted to take Emil off the job because he had 31 years' service, and had been on his job 13 years. Emil still had six years to go for retirement. Until then, no progress was possible.

Then a curious thing happened. Another listener interrupted: "One of our superintendents is just like that—only his name is Charlie." Then followed a whole chorus of interruptions. Everyone, it seemed, knew in his own company a superintendent, a manager, or a foreman who fitted the description of Emil.

So, Emil is everywhere, only his name is something else. But . . . is this a fate or a problem? Is no progress possible, or is the need only to find a solution which fits Emil?

I have met Emil in many plants. *From him, from his bosses, from his associates, and from his subordinates I have learned much about him and his attitudes, including his attitude toward quality.*

Curiously enough, Emil would rather make good products than bad ones. He likes to have it said of him that "Emil does a good job." Emil would rather have a high rate of yield than a low rate, because then he can meet his delivery schedules easier. Emil would rather have his men make high earnings than lose those earnings in rework. I have never met a production head named Emil or otherwise who preferred bad work to good work.

The Emils I have met have some other things in common. Out of a long career with the company, they can recall many pleasant memories but also some bitter ones. Here and there they have endured an uninspiring boss, a siege of unwarranted blame, or a piece of skullduggery from some industrial adventurer who tried to rush through in two months what takes a year or two to mature.

Emil looks to these experiences for much guidance to meet the problems ahead. He is getting on in years and he is slowing up. No longer does he consider it a calamity if he is passed up for promotion. But it would be a real calamity if he should be blamed for some big failure, and risk losing the status he already has.

It took Emil many years to become a superintendent. Most of the fellows he started with are still on the machine or on the bench. In their eyes, and in his own eyes, he has arrived.

Emil is reconciled to the idea that he will probably never get to be manager. Younger fellows have already passed him up in enough numbers to make this clear. The big thing, for Emil, is not to lose his job as superintendent. The young superintendents are of a different mind. The last thing they want is to remain a superintendent all their life. They can afford to gamble and take chances with new ways. But Emil is too far along in years and in service to dare to gamble.

So Emil uses the utmost caution to protect his flank. His security is not threatened one bit by the usual day-to-day fires he must put out. He has been doing that for many years, and knows how to cope with the day-to-day problems. Any threat to his security will not come from these familiar problems, but from something which is to him unfamiliar and untried.

This brings us to the heart of the problem of dealing with the "obstructionist." Emil is going to "obstruct" whatever is a threat to his security. He would not be human if he acted otherwise. The problem in dealing with Emil is "simply" to avoid a threat to Emil's security.

For some engineers this is all wrong. They are advocating something that is so logical (to them) and so valuable to the company (in their opinion). Why should this not be adopted forthwith? Why is it necessary to act out a game with Emil, to cater to his whims, to make it seem that it is really his ideas which are being put into effect?

In particular the engineers reproach their own top management. Emil, they say, should be ordered to put these new ideas into effect. Yet this suggestion by the engineers betrays shocking ignorance of the fundamental rules of organization. If top management is to hold Emil responsible for results, it must give him collateral authority to decide to act. To order him to adopt this or that new proposal would be taking away with the left hand the authority top management gave Emil with its right hand.

So there is no escape from selling Emil himself on the ideas. If the engineers could only grasp this fact! Once they put their minds to it, they could discover many devices for selling; in fact, they could borrow them intact from other heads in their own company. If they make their first job that of convincing Emil that they are no threat to his security, they have crossed the real barrier.

My own rule for judging whether Emil is going to be a problem is to discover whether Emil has (a) integrity, and (b) common sense. If these things are present, the limitations on results lie only in the sales ability of the engineers".

CHAPTER 9

The Pitfalls of *Scientism*

When a distinguished but elderly scientist states that something is possible, he is almost certainly right. When he states that something is impossible, he is very probably wrong.[1]

—Arthur C. Clarke

To make a system robust you have to design freedom into it. Individual choice confers a survival advantage that ants don't have. That's why men are going to Mars while ants are still building holes in the ground. God knew what He was doing. Stalin did not.[2]

—Richard Fernandez

Scientism is a comb-over of the ancient *Appeal to Authority* fallacy. It grants special privilege to claims expressed in empirical jargon, but which are not *falsifiable*. This ranks high among the failure modes that sap sustainment.

F.W. Taylor's *"scientific management"* was *scientism* for industry. This 1910s movement for reductionism-in-labor displaced system-thinking. It was embraced as the "progressive" model for industrial engineering education and the employment of human labor. Behold Taylor's own summary of this principle:

It is only through enforced standardization of methods . . . implements and working conditions, and enforced cooperation that this faster work can be assured. And the duty of enforcing the adoption of standards and enforcing this cooperation rests with management alone.[3]

Enforced cooperation is quite the oxymoron. The caste system it erected between doers and bosses only started getting chiseled back in earnest since the 1980s quality revolution. Much work still remains if we are to repair the breaches of mutuality in problem-solving.

Those concerned with *who's right* over *what's right* dress up social agendas in costumes of tech and statistics, to set them above reach of dispute. *Scientistic* assertion of authority is alive and well in the credentialing industry, where captains of enterprise receive their formation.

Karl Popper's upbringing in pre-war Vienna personally acquainted him with the works of Adler, Freud, Marx, and the like. He saw the great sway of empirical sophistry. He wrote *The Logic of Scientific Discovery* to help sincere learners maintain distinctions. This is the twentieth century's key source on the idea of science itself. Until and unless we grasp it, we will remain unable to comprehend *kata* and the rule-set.

It is tempting to give our side's ideas a pass, by short-cutting the burden of trial by the formal scientific method. This is *scientistic* fallacy. It is tempting to lend the cachet and implied rigor of numerical expressions to propositions that lie outside the purview of science. Social propositions borrow an air of respectability by arguing in the "objective" language of "hard" sciences. This kind of signaling for leverage is *scientistic* fallacy.

Science owes no apology to the liberal arts, and the liberal arts owe no apology to science. Any dichotomy between the two is a false one: Breakthrough in complexity requires critical thinking, and the ability to choose the investigative tool appropriate to the question at hand.

Popper wished to distinguish pseudo-science from actual science. It wouldn't help to simplistically recommend that we just follow a party or the side who is "right": Sometimes scientists are wrong, and sometimes pseudo-science luckily stumbles into true observations. Science is not distinguished by its reams of empirical observation and techy equations. The superstition of astrology has just as many of those as does the science of astronomy. Popper insisted that,

> We ought to try as hard as we can to overthrow our solution, rather than defend it. Few of us, unfortunately, practise this precept. . . . [others] fortunately, will supply the criticism for us if we fail to supply it ourselves.[4]

Hmm . . . a feedback loop. . . . Risky.

Popper saw in Einstein's work a character fundamentally different from the kind of claims by Marx, Freud, and Adler. Einstein held the moral courage to go on record with risky, non-obvious predictions that were possible to disprove.

If his gravitational theory was so, light must get bent in passing by a dense mass. This was not something that could normally be observed—starlight is hidden in broad daylight. But by measuring nighttime position of a star, and repeating during solar eclipse, we would either confirm or falsify his risky, non-obvious prediction.

Scientism: Appeals to authority. Technological and statistical forms are employed with the purpose of lending an air of credibility to a proposition.

Science: By making non-obvious, risky predictions, I attempt to engineer *falsification* of my own proposition. If unable to break it, I go use it with earned confidence.

Where contextual conditions are met, the *scientific method* is a most effective way to spare us the falsity of beliefs that contain hidden conditionals. Integrity led Popper to distinguish real science in a famous formulation[5]:

- It is easy to confirm our hypothesis . . . if we look for confirmations. It only counts if it is the result of a risky prediction.
- Every "good" theory is a prohibition. The more a theory forbids, the better.
- Confirming evidence should not count except when it is the result of a genuine but unsuccessful attempt to *falsify* the theory.

Hayek calls it *blind ambition*, pretense and posing, when we carry on with empirical and numerical affectations in contexts where the prerequisites of science are unmet. Many questions in the social sciences are so. Aspects in complexity suffer this also (see in the next chapter). As Hayek put it,

The blind transfer of the striving for quantitative measurements to a field in which the specific conditions are not present which give it its basic importance in the natural sciences, is the result of an entirely unfounded prejudice.[6]

Here are three final keys from Popper's formulation of what makes something "scientific":

- That which is not refutable by any conceivable event is nonscientific. This does not make it untrue, but it does make it unscientific.
- Irrefutability is not a virtue (as often thought). A genuine test is an attempt to *falsify*.
- Some, when falsified, reinterpret events ad hoc in a way that sidesteps refutation and holds onto pride and reputation. This vacates their scientific status.

The *scientistic* as distinguished from the scientific view is not an unprejudiced but a very prejudiced approach which, before it has considered its subject, claims to know what is the most appropriate way of investigating it.[7]

Fall from Rule-Connection, Back into End-Connection, "Because Science"

When the scientist stresses that he studies objective facts he means. . . . The views people hold about the external world are to him always a stage to be overcome.[8]

It is not possible to weigh the unexpected and social consequence of a plan, *independent of the beliefs of the affected about this arrangement we have in mind.* How (if) it may align with their several aims IS the issue of **mutuality**. The social sciences are what the affected perceive, and wish to do at the intersections. We investigate with rigor. But so as not to abuse the limits of science, we must bring resourceful ways to handle the uncertain, the unknown, and the unknowable. Stay tuned for **Part 3**.

Science is great at cracking naturalistic cause-effect type questions.

It may not exactly fit some others we face: Unintended – social consequences, mutuality, un-foreseeable bifurcation of complexity.

These don't lend to non-obvious, falsifiable prediction, the *démarche* of science.

Right Tool for the Job?

Lean takes up and puts away tools like disposable appliances, means to an end. Science is one of many. Hayek, Popper, and Juran focused the back-half of their careers on helping us to right the abuse of technical tools and better-choosing the right ones for the job at hand.

To reap the windfall of rule-connection is to get the actors to jointly seek points of mutuality, for peer extension where they intersect. The leader question is how to earn the *consent of the governed* to that pursuit. This is the hard but effective, durable way to order an enterprise.

Knowers seem to think there is a straighter way to the end: Revert the group to end-connection. This kind of leadership forms and directs the group to a common (enforced) aim. We experts just *know* what that aim needs to be. Once we have pitched it at the town hall, how soon can we just get on with it? Each expert personality goes about this in their own style—to be inspiring, likeable, expert, or through straight-up compulsion and fear. Not so much literacy, but numeracy is the language favored in these kinds of directives.

Bottom line, *scientism* is not about getting the laity to search out mutuality and extend; it is bending them to comply and extend my design. This is a backslide from rule-connection back to end-connection. End-connection can't extend so far or so fast as can emergence. The laity eventually see through it, and it turns management into a story of them-versus-us.

Scientistic thinking lies at the core of resistance, backsliding, and failure to sustain.

CHAPTER 10

The Pitfalls of Complexity

A shift to a new niche or adaptive zone requires, almost without exception, a change in behavior.[1]

—Ernst Mayr

Breakthrough is the fundamental change in our paradigm of what is "normal" around here. It comes after our catalog of institutional answers is exhausted by complexity.

A Simple System

A gardener pots a seed, which lies dormant in winter, then springs up into a daisy.

C A U S E

Final Cause is a man's purpose to show his wife that he thinks of her often.

Formal Cause is his plan, to express it with a live daisy, on her desk.

Material Cause is potting soil, light, water, time, and a seed.

Efficient Cause is a man who tends, and the sun which supplies photons.

Cause precedes effect.[2]

A Complicated System

A daisy is a simple system. Scaling up to four, or to a field of daisies, *complicates* this system. It is still seed, soil, water, light, and care—just on a wider stage. Tending a field is more complicated than a single stem, but it's the same system, writ large.

In complicated systems individuals function somewhat independently. Adding agents amounts to scaling or proportioning. Removing one of the actors doesn't rewrite the behavior of the rest. Only those in direct contact could tell the difference if one were taken.

1 daisy	4 daisies	Photosynthesis:
$6\ CO_2 + 6\ H_2O \rightarrow C_6H_{12}O_6 + 6\ O_2$	$24\ CO_2 + 24\ H_2O \rightarrow 4\ C_6H_{12}O_6 + 24\ O_2$	

x1 **x4** capturing solar energy

IN CO_2 CO_2 CO_2 CO_2 CO_2 to transform CO_2 and H_2O

into sugar for food

$C_6H_{12}O_6$ glucose $C_6H_{12}O_6$ $C_6H_{12}O_6$ $C_6H_{12}O_6$ $C_6H_{12}O_6$

OUT

O_2 O_2 O_2 O_2 O_2 O_2 by-product

Reductionism[3] is experts' old go-to for tackling enterprise-level issues. *How do you eat an elephant? One bite at a time*, is the mentality. No matter how gigantic the system, improving it is said to be cut down to size by zooming in to meticulously master each of the component parts. As each local unit gets improved, it is imagined to roll up as increased output on the whole.

Here lies Taylorism—ambition to subdivide aims into elemental tasks, on down to relentless micro-mastery of those. Dividing and conquering—if we only go far enough and deep enough—is thought to push improvement through the whole. This might be arguable—*if* interactions in our complex systems were negligible. But there is the rub.

Complexity's Interactions: More Cause Than Effect

I have led many "scale-ups"—assembly, chemical, logistic, planning, and administrative. Many of my bosses project-managed to the expectation of a proportional outcome. I don't recall even one that scaled linearly— modern means are a complex bundle.

In complexity, it's not the triggers—it's the interactions—that cause outcomes. Evolutionary **causation runs backwards** from our conventional notion of cause and effect . . . functional effects **are** the causal 'mechanisms'.[4]

Yes, something does facilitate a meeting. A bus drops a visiting football team at an opponent's campus. But it is *interaction* of offense against a defense on the field—not the bus trip—that causes a score to emerge. A forfeit is a tribal affair—no interaction and no score.

Triggers cause interactions—but they can't simplistically be said to cause the effect. Cause does precede effect, but it may not always look that way. It is easy to spot triggers, but interactions stay unseen unless teased out by the scientific method. A characteristic of complex systems is that often cause and effect appear to run backwards. The *analysis* we learned at school is reductionism, predicated on a linear chain of cause-effect–secondary cause-effect–tertiary cause-effect, and so on down the line.

A complex system is not linear: It is comprised of stocks, flows, and feedback loops. The feedback loops often make effect appear to precede cause. It is the tool of *synthesis* rather than analysis that affords a view on this aspect of complexity. A flowchart is analysis: It is reasoning from the particulars to the general. A Value Stream Map is synthesis: It is reasoning from the general to the particulars. To effectively extend order and sustain it, we look both ways.

The Driving Force in Emergence

Self-arranging systems like *Takt Attainment* run on causal *kata* embedded at the intersections ahead of time, as order-favoring connection modes. Times of change release this stored energy (information) to effect action repertoires that appear self-ordering, running uphill.

Dependencies-linkages-hidden conditionals shape the behavior of complex systems. Removing an agent affects far beyond the neighbors in direct contact. In sorting cause from effect, what matters is not so much the proximate cause that triggered the system: It is the released behavioral *inter*-actions (*kata*) that fuel the assembly of new structure.

> Dissecting a complexity as if it were an additive collection denatures it by unhooking its causal intersections. Legos have interlocking interfaces that don't presuppose a final structure but do promote literal extension in novel configurations. Dominoes are similar blocks, but they don't interlock. Stacking of Legos is complex. It invites extension into surprising outcomes. A column of dominoes is complicated—just additive.
>
> If we change interest from static stacking to dynamic tumbling, dominoes are a complex system. Remove one from a spaced line of dominoes and the rest are affected. Here spacing is the "how" of interface. Pushing a first domino is a trigger. It can be called cause, but only in a context of deliberate spacing invested at the intersections, ahead of time.
>
> Strategic complexity is to engineer how actors interface. Reductionist complication is scale, minus or plus. Improvement fails to sustain where we naively piecemeal complex modules as if they were just plug-and-play complications of scale.

> Evolutionists have tended to focus on a particular factor, or 'selection pressure', or on the functional properties of a new 'gene' . . . . in fact **the dynamics of evolutionary causation is always interactional and relational.**[5]

> Corning recalls the familiar example of genetic differences in lighter-versus-darker strains of peppered moths, in this light. Their proportions in the English countryside famously adapted during the Industrial Revolution.
>
> Moth color differences mattered because soot blackened the bark of trees where the moths lit. That mattered because the moths were subject to predators who located them visually. The "mechanism" responsible for the population shift in peppered moths was the *interaction* between moth color, tree-trunk color, and the type of predators in the area. Had bats been the worry (echo not visual

location), or oil rather than coal the fuel, one would hear approximately zero about peppered moths in high school science.

Any factor that precipitates change in the interaction behavior of actors and environment represents potential release of a complex's stored potential to up-fit its own complexity.

> It is very often the new habit which sets up the selection pressure that shifts the mean . . . the importance of behavior in initiating new evolutionary events is self-evident. . . . Changes of evolutionary significance are rarely . . . the direct result of mutation pressure.[6]

Rodgers and Hammerstein could choreograph the most efficient standard work dance ever. As a standalone work, it would amount only to "mutation pressure." Our experts will amount to just one more voice striving to be heard over the rivalrous noise of a complex workplace. Daily, distracted experts pass by millions of discoveries, unaware, or out of bandwidth.

Breakthrough rises above noise where behavioral shift pace-makes. Behavior shift evokes dormant and unperceived conditionals and interaction modes, no expert required. Institutions of "standard" and standard work must culturally appropriate this pace-making. We will recall this in Part III countermeasures for sustainment.

Joint Testing of Differences as "Pacemaker"

Joint testing of rivalrous alternatives among the stakeholders institutionalizes behavioral shifts. Testing of standard work alternatives in a forward-running loop unlocks the kind of interactions and hidden conditionals that fuel breakthrough and sustainment in groups.

Consensus is the art of deliberately surfacing where we disagree, so that we can agree which of the rival ideas we will go test.

In *The Skilled Facilitator*, Roger Schwarz has written the peerless how-to guide for the leadership *kata* of **mutual learning**.[7] See especially the section *Jointly Design Next Steps*.

Forward-looping PDCA—rivalrous, recombinant adaptation of the standard work *kata*—is the behavioral key that unlocks breakthrough in value-adding operations.

Reason Restored to Its Rightful Place

It is a service, not an attack on reason, to criticize how hubris deformed the 20th century by undoing the causal intersections of frontliners, specialists, experts, and management.

Pretence of Knowledge was Hayek's Nobel acceptance lecture. He singled out mutual learning as our stiffest challenge. To do more good than harm, those with power must learn:

> In complexity no leader can acquire the extent and circumstantial depth of knowledge needed to control events. Leaders can't prescribe and synthesize an outcome—but good ones can know how to find it through favorable interactions.
>
> We are not so much builders of complexity as its gardeners, or physicians: We don't synthesize food (order) out of atoms; we find, plant, and care-take the thing out of which it emerges. Across the span of the value stream we facilitate the sorts of interfaces, known of sifted experience, that favor order's extending itself.
>
> A value stream from seed to the table is much wider than the competence of an expert.

> recognition of the insuperable **limits to his knowledge ought indeed to teach . . . humility** which should guard him against becoming . . . destroyer of a civilization which no brain has designed but which has grown from the free efforts of millions.[9]

Ad Fontes

Many rules are done as patches, not as the adaptations of system they need to be. It is easy to reply with regulation to pacify a crisis at a unit. Just living to fight another day aggravates and increases the complexity of system whole. Long term, this adds to improvement woes.

Simplicity without being simplistic, to serve and be responsive in ways that keep complexity of the whole in mind, takes mindfulness. This is the good road, not the easiest. Sustainment requires that we see improvement as a process, not as an event.

Complexity brings us to see our doings more as *countermeasures*. To call them *solutions* is presumptuous, in light of what we cannot know.

Law, Legislation, and Liberty is the definitive resource on how to reform a rule-set, recover simplicity, and sustain effectiveness. The companion *Constitution of Liberty* (particularly Chapter 2) exposits what makes the infrastructure of standard work tick (daily improvement boards, walkabouts, etc.).

To debunk *scientistic* technocracy is not a suggestion that *anarchy* or sentiment would be better in its place. Lean *restores* the preeminence of reason, by demanding mutual learning of *all* stakeholders, not just ones called elite. *Catallaxy* rejoins the fragmentary, partial knowledge of a learning multitude, by reforming the causal intersections that get denatured by the overreach of knowers.

> Reason undoubtedly is man's most precious possession . . . [what] we have attempted is a defense of reason, against its abuse by those who do not understand the conditions of its effective functioning and continuous growth.[10]

Hayek and Popper took great pains to discredit *scientistic* fallacy. Their argument was against monopolistic supervision that inhibits continual pursuit of better. Against complexity the enterprise needs all hands on deck—every person-process-day. Their argument was with elites who so underestimate complexity as to presume that they comprehend and direct it.

Reductionism Is Totally Inadequate Viewpoint to Lead in Complexity

In 1893 The Tiffany Chapel graced the Chicago World's Fair.

This feat of complexity now crowns the Morse Museum of Modern Art in Winter Park, Florida.

A PhD on silica, another in refractory, another in colorimetry, another in visual arts...

... Subatomic analysis of sand with light could not tell us the artist's meta-intent of aesthetics and worldview.

Each tile is many grains of sand. The altar alone contains 150,000 handmade tiles, 3-tiles deep.

It is a view on the whole that comprehends the roles of individual tiles in this complexity.

Statistical Aggregate Is No View of Complex Enterprise

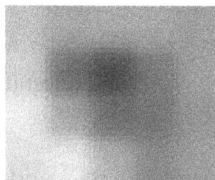

A photo, at 2 pixels per inch.	The same photo, at 5 pixels per inch.	The same photo, at 300 pixels per inch -

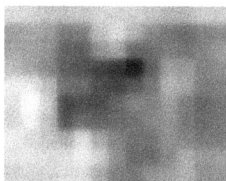

waiting for the most exciting 25-seconds in college football.

We need the pixels—especially the interactions—to relate a complex whole. Reductionism fails to explain, and mostly fails to improve, a complexity.

If Greek science had been less deductive and less ridden by dogma, heliocentric astronomy might have begun its development eighteen centuries earlier than it did.[11]

PART 3

System-Thinking— Consequently—Behavioral Routines to Extend Improvement

Part 3: Systematizes our approach to that which promotes the re-extension of gain.

System-think informs the sort of improvement that sustains. On it, we form up action routines, as in-context countermeasures against nature's drivers to attrition.

CHAPTER 11

Breakthrough in How We See Others

We cannot be guided in our practical action by full knowledge and evaluation of all the consequences. So long as men are not omniscient, the only way in which freedom can be given to the individual is by such general rules to delimit the sphere in which the decision is his.[1]

—F.A. Hayek

If the question still sounds natural with "You idiot" at its end, don't ask it.[2]

—Roger Schwarz

The convictions of another are what they are persuaded of, not what I insist. I may influence. But their paradigms form up in a place outside of what I can presume to control.

Most of what it takes to tilt our intersections to mutuality is something that does fall within my control. We can't make others think a thing. But we can model how to extend our several aims through complementary effort. Toward sustainment, we do well to remember this.

"The Use of Knowledge in Society"

Hayek's 1945 article took only a few pages to politely, thoroughly debunk the overreach of *scientific management*. It fundamentally reformed paradigms of management, planning, control, and the stunning extensions of information science we enjoy ever since.

Colleges prepare us to work **the engineering problem**—enterprise-scale *reductionism*: "Given" an inventory of resources —"given" their properties—"given" definition of performance, and response curves for all uses—one could reduce society to mass calculation. Engineers work to organize the "givens" to compute the optimal arrangement of resources. It is then down to experts to plan and for workers to do. That's nice and all, but inventory, utility, and response are not "given" in a real-world enterprise.

In complexity, the inputs, outputs, and tradeoffs are many, transient, and purely circumstantial. Resources substitute 10^{xx} ways down a value stream, as do outcomes. Use of any, instantly denies a portion to others that they could count on only moments ago. Time continually shuffles the gigantic, global array of substitution ratios. So, how to plan and control?

Cowboy Up: Try to Process All of It?

The information required to plan exists in bits, dispersed, not centrally observable and actionable. Current inventory, and alternative uses open to us, are only observable at all the separate *gembas* in one, shared instant. Our expert can only be at one or zero of those.

Locals can't encode in numbing detail. We couldn't transmit it all if they had. Planning couldn't process it all, compute, and return equally detailed instruction, timely, to all *gembas*. By the time locals could decode and do in detail, "optimum" will have fled away. There is no escape: To sustain and extend order, the front-liners are going to have to be counted upon to steward the *knowledge of the circumstances of time and place*, for reflexive action on the spot:

> unique information of which beneficial use might be made, but . . . only if the decisions depending on it are left to him [the local] or are made with his active cooperation.[3]

While we are highlighting experts' inadequacy, let's admit to our own: What can be known on-the-spot is partial, often contradictory, fleeting. Locals can see only soil, bark, rain, leaves, maybe whole trees—but are in no position to "see the forest for the trees."

Optimum uses *circumstances of time and place*—all details—of all trees—over the whole forest—all at once. It is a paradox: We need a macro that contains full-spectrum micro. No expert or board can do both/all. Here is how *dense heterarchy* runs circles around *anarchy*, militant individualism, tribalism, and top-down *hierarchy*.

OK, What If We Simplify Complexity to the Point It Is Calculable?

Extent of circumstances overwhelm ability to encode, transmit, trade off, and instruct, in time. Experts don't easily give up on expert control. Their next play is to render planning calculations manageable, by summing great reams of local specifics into a few statistical aggregates, KPI.

> lumping together, as resources of one kind, **items which differ** as regards location, quality, and other particulars, **in a way which may be very significant** for the specific decision.[4]

But knowledge of circumstantial differences is the distinctive that positions us to exploit, to do better than "normal." Gainful openings and notable risks all get blended together into invisibility in an average, sent onward for use. If my feet are in snow and my hair in a campfire, do I average out to feel like a happy camper?

Macro planning based on aggregates overgeneralizes. It is too blunt an instrument to optimize the *gemba* tactically. It is abstinence from opportunistic use of circumstantial detail. It is institutionalized reversion to the mean—*Just Say No* to the fleetingly exceptional.

Firms don't roll up averages because it sharpens decisions. They do it because experts are forced to settle, to get calculation possible at all. Macro is like searching for keys under a streetlight because it's where we can see, not in the dark over where we dropped them.

Reflexive Planning Is More Efficient

Hayek illustrated reflexive control with the example of tin. Say somewhere, an invention or popularity causes a run on the use of tin . . . or . . . somewhere a key supplier suffers outage.

The end-users have no idea where and why. They do know shelves are bare, and price is up for what they do find: That information suffices.

Their unfilled *kanban* wordlessly announce that it is in their interest to economize on tin. This can mean creatively using less. Or substituting other materials. Or pulling cash from less preferred activities, to outbid our rivals and keep getting tin. The signal tells users to rearrange their activities. It points up *how* to start interacting at their junctions, *but not what* to do. That depends on circumstance, and the skill they can muster to exploit it.

Systems like pull, markets, and traffic circles connect us. In times of change they join dissimilar strangers into orthogonal thinking and behavior shift in response. If the tie is mutuality, very resourceful solutions emerge from unexpected directions.

Conditions telegraph the circumstantial opportunity beyond users, to suppliers. They don't need to know why, only of unfilled *kanban*, and premiums users may offer. They might bring capacity online, prioritize this outlet for their tin over other less fulfilling ones, creatively unlock supplies that were assumed unavailable and so forth.

Conditions telegraph circumstantial opportunity beyond users and suppliers, to substitutes. They perceive an opening to substitute steel, or aluminum, paper, plastics. Or plastic lids, sparing tin for walls. Or recycle. Or new shapes that stiffen for thickness reduction.

The rule-set does not prescribe how. It shapes behaviors that incentivize opportunistic reconnecting, invention, to re-form order where we intersect. "How" is entrusted to creativity of actors bound by mutuality, to explore circumstantial advantage in answer to the signals of *kanban* and price. Substitution affects the substitution ratios of all the substitutes, which adjusts substitutes' substitutes, substitutes' substitutes for substitutes' substitutes—all the way down the line. The extended value stream reassembles itself in *catallaxy*:

> not because any of its members survey the whole field, but because their limited individual fields of vision sufficiently overlap so that through many intermediaries the relevant information is communicated to all.[5]

Kanban and *Takt* speak this within the firm. Price does it at the interfaces on either end—down the extended value streams of supply and dispatch.

> The mere fact that there is one price for any commodity—or rather that local prices are connected . . . brings about **the solution which . . . is in fact dispersed among all the people involved** in the process.[6]

Takt within, and price without, are civilization's most efficient form of:

> telecommunications which enables individual producers to watch merely the movement of a few pointers . . . to adjust their activities to changes of which they may never know more than is reflected in the price movement.[7]

Solutions Are Fragmentary and Dispersed

Once we grasp that information is fragmentary, it dawns that **answers are dispersed**. This transforms thinking on the role of others, with whom we intersect.

> facts are never so given to a single mind . . . it is necessary that in the **solution of the problem** knowledge should be used that **is dispersed among many people**.[8]

In light of the limitations of expertise, the question is not if but *how* to plan. *Control had been a paradigm of how to gather dispersed knowledge, to narrow the span of who holds it*, sufficiently that an expert can reconcile it all. In the *scientistic* view, planning is how to gather, compute, and dispense for a great many others to execute. Then—*eureka*—it dawns on us that solutions are dispersed. The idea of planning is reshaped:

> **how to extend the span** of our utilization of resources **beyond the span of the control of any one mind** . . . to provide inducements which will make the individuals do the desirable things without anyone having to tell them.[9]

For breakthrough in planning, the question is how to disperse it among the actors, not gather it up from them into a directorial basket.

Breakthrough in how we see (rely on) others lies at the heart of whether we can sustain. *The Use of Knowledge in Society* is a guide for that journey.

> Any approach . . . [like MRP's push scheduling of multiple assets in parallel] which in effect starts from the assumption that people's knowledge corresponds with the objective facts of the situation, systematically leaves out what is our main task to explain.[10]

Kuhn Complements Hayek's Insight

Structure of Scientific Revolutions adds further insight into how to navigate the paradigms among us, where they become irreconcilable. Kuhn's insight on incommensurability is key to *breakthrough in how we see others*.

Incommensurability

Wherever people have a go at breaking through, first off they try to extend paradigms that were already useful in other situations. Eventually they run up against things they fail to explain, a crisis of expertise. New concepts arise to fill the void. The tug-of-war over rival paradigms plays more like fighting over faith conversion, than considerate inquiry or reconciling of differences. This is *incommensurability* of views.

Kuhn sums up crystal clear how deeply held convictions affect learning and change. He catalogues what we are up against, to break through with, not in spite of, those around us:

- We can't make others embrace a new view in one stroke of cold, unassailable logic:
  The establishment is almost never entirely discredited and stupid. Relativity displaced the mechanics scientists used since the 1600s. Even so, we still learn Newtonian physics: It is useful within context. Once it explained enough to be the establishment. No one then presumed it was perfect. Let's not pretend now that it did not serve remarkably. It owns a record, unlike new ideas that

are still morphing. Where the old still explains, it seems fair to ask what's in it for users to switch paradigms. Rarely was every aspect of an old idea irredeemably evil.

The new is still under construction—never *"settled"*. It doesn't yet carry the pedigree of its rivals. It holds promise where tested so far. But some domains yet remain to be filled in. Rarely if ever were all aspects of a new wave as pure as the wind-driven snow.

- People can't swap in gradual stages from one *incommensurable* mindset to another.

   An old paradigm and its replacement are usually irreconcilable. Without dissolving into a walking, mental contradiction, people find it hard to hold two opposing worldviews at once. *You can't be partially pregnant.* Paradigms are quantum steps. Once it does go, paradigm shift runs like a conversion.

   We can't force in one stroke, but they can't embrace in a string of half-measures, either. Thus, we come to Kuhn's advice in this quandary:

- Stop trying to dress up perfect truth claims to overwhelm the *"deniers"*.

   Forget propositional shock and awe—to learners it looks like a great white whale, and you look like Captain Ahab. Few issues yield across the board to one inarguable new answer. It is counterproductive to persecute as heretics those who disagree. If we lose grip on mutuality it sets our view on the bad side of credibility, to all who watch. It sets a change agent's motives on the wrong side of vetting. It undoes persuasion.

In navigating irreconcilable views we can't control what objectors think. We can control what we think. So, how can self-satisfied leaders from the old school be brought to switch? Here is Kuhn's wise advice:

Countermeasures to Intransigence

- **Accept reality**—many won't come over: Their paradigm may retire when they do.
- **Settle for tolerance.** For now, pursue **persuasion** over **proof**.

Hasten the demise of the outdated idea, not its proponents. Proof develops over time, in processes not events. Expand it along the way. *Catallaxy* is tolerance—a form of acceptance confident enough that it needs to neither yield nor demand acquiescence. Co-adaptation repudiates the arrogance that equates progress to having submitted the neighbors to my aims. We need only bind ourselves by a simple, abstract, mutually favorable rule-set equal for all.

- **Find islands and bridgeheads**—domains where the new paradigm can test in ways that require only local embrace, not immediate, mass conversion.
  Sustainment does not set out to build arguments that conquer, but rather the kind of community that always eventually recognizes payoff in reconnecting to extend, at least where interests intersect.

  > Paradigm debates are not really about comparative problem-solving ability . . . the issue is which paradigm should guide research on next problems, many of which neither side can yet claim to resolve completely.[11]

- **Leapfrog:** Use the paradigm to conquer valuable things that are as-yet unsolved.
- **Snowball little cascades of professional affinities** instead of universal salvation.
- **Clinically expose what are genuine gaps in the current paradigm.**

Maintain healthy distance from conniving and *schadenfreude.*

But **fully dismantle all insulation from between elites and the workaday realities that confront the laity. Leader Standard Work** is the most powerful, practical means to this end. We will unpack this in the next chapter.

The above has been great advice for when others are holding back breakthrough. But let's be fair—sometimes *I* am the holdup. This brings us to the next chapter—breakthrough in how I see my own self.

CHAPTER 12

Breakthrough in How We See Ourselves

O wad some Pow'r the giftie gie us, To see oursels as ithers see us!
—Robert Burns

The uneducated . . . cannot be expected to be self-critical.[1]
—Socrates

Why Do We Need Leaders?

It has little to do with motivational style or which reporting structure can best gather say-so into the hands of stars and experts. Leadership supercharges operational performance *because it is a special case of division of labor and specialization*—the one that makes flow possible against the headwinds of complexity.

- Of all the ways we could service demand, flow consumes the least treasure per unit output. Not-flow is an exceptionally draining way to operate.
  - Demand flow is hard, but the socioeconomic advantages are extraordinary. It optimally connects and arranges utility of actors and resources on the spot. Value is neither interrupted nor stagnated in pools of backwash. Compromise on this feature trades away advantages rapidly.
- Complexity stretches service realization inter-*spatially*, inter-*temporally*, inter-*personally*:
  - Once complexity drives the person-hours of work content beyond the tipping point of demand rate (*Takt*), it takes multiple

persons to achieve delivery time. It turns formerly simple streams of material, labor, and information parallel and interpersonal.

○ Complexity means more items to differentiate, until brought into the complex at the right moment, oriented onto a spot. This amplifies space and upkeep demands. This obliges value-adders to overwatch a wider span, all within *Takt* frequency of end-delivery of a unit of value to customer.

○ Most value-aiding support tasks build over timeframes much longer than Takt. Intersections, handoffs, and shared tasks multiply in complexity. Front-liners are asked to assist in value-aiding needs out-of-cycle, and cover some of the extended physical span. On the next breath we challenge them to subordinate these, to get back available to discharge in-cycle duties punctually at Takt.

Leaders' Service

All value-adding duty generates need for out-of-cycle **value-aiding service**. It entails:

1. **Alignment of purpose**—*Telos*—my own purposes, and facilitating others' at the intersections
2. **Resource attainment**
3. **Transmission and communication of information**
4. **Compliance and containment**

Complexity stretches value-aiding services out over a span or duration wider than an actor can loop through at *Takt*. Duties come to surpass demand rate. Multiple agents therefore are needed to share the burden in parallel, for delivery time to be achievable. If not, flow is broken, and problems and costs multiply.

It is economically compelling to externalize and subordinate out-of-cycle activities: This way, value-aiding does not undo value-adding flow. Supervision offered in aid to value-add is that special case of specialization that makes flow possible in the face of complexity. The socioeconomic payoff is explosive.

Leadership **externalizes** key out-of-cycle needs from value-add:

1. **Purpose alignment—*Telos***

   Tactics like *stigmergy* propel groups efficiently. But minus a **meta-agenda**—the overarching purpose—we corkscrew like unguided heat-seeking missiles. Heaven only knows where we may end up, but count on engineers and accountants to boast how efficiently we got there.

   We need strategy—not inline, but an out-of-cycle specialized service. Leadership is provided to deliver this service.

2. **Resource attainment**

   Two aspects of resourcing specialization make up the bulk of leader activity

   - Fetch the value-adders the means they need to do [**SCQDP**]

     Safely, in **C**ompliance, produce **Q**uality, **D**elivered on-time, **P**roductively

   - Expose and remove barriers that hinder it

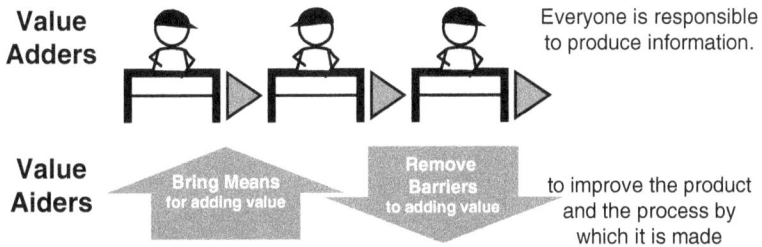

Value Adders — Everyone is responsible to produce information.

Value Aiders — Bring Means for adding value — Remove Barriers to adding value — to improve the product and the process by which it is made

3. **Transmission and communication of information**

   To be a going concern, every operation requires two kinds of information:

Stored Knowledge	Knowledge of Circumstances of Time and Place
transmitted	*communicated*
down through time	punctually across the span of cooperation
crystallized, stored as Rule Set, referentials, moral code	**fragmentary, dispersed** among all stakeholders: transient, situational opportunity or challenge
participants maintain learning, not eternally condemned to re-learn same lessons over and over	participants exploit circumstance by *kata* of mutual self-rearrangement into form that promotes extension of order, on the spot

This formulation by Hayek neatly sums up the use of knowledge in society, quite literally that which fuels civilization. Leadership is what elevates strategy above mere tactics that produce action but no information. It arouses operations out of the dead symbolism of strategies that would beautify dashboards of information but effect no action.

4. **Compliance and Containment**

Some fraction of people act antisocially (incapable, unwilling), fraying mutuality. At the interfaces across their span of control, leaders go out and uphold the bounds of the rule-set, ensuring that such do not abuse the dignity, rights, and property of other stakeholders.

> Mankind achieved civilization by developing and learning to follow rules . . . that often forbade him to do what his instincts demanded . . . Means to prevent clashes between conflicting aims and not a set of fixed ends.[2]

Where a rule-set needs to evolve or be enforced, leaders see to it through amendment and information, not *anarchy* or at the expense of flow. The best division of labor is context-driven.

Arranging as described by Russ Scaffede and J.M. Juran is a sensible start:

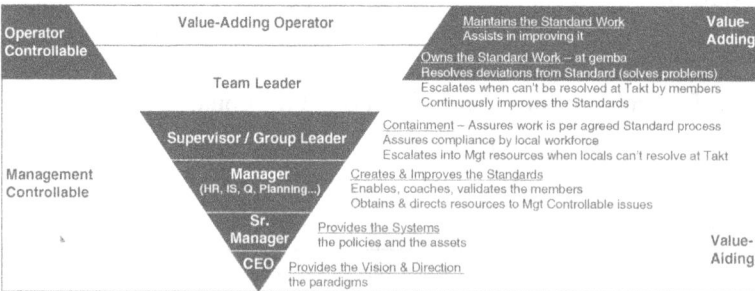

Specialization tends to harden into *hierarchy*. It clings to reward based on who gets to administer rules. It incentivizes specialists to obstruct new arrangements for improvement.

The antidote is a culture of **servant leadership** that is clear on what is value-add versus **value-subtraction**. Complex enterprise runs best if roles adapt on pull of mutuality. *Dense heterarchy* attaches leadership to context, not personality.[3] This builds in a natural counter to the excesses of *hierarchy*.

The direction should make special effort to tie reward to facilitation of value-add, not to who holds the rule book or the number of headcount they direct. Metrics and reward must align with meta-agenda, else mutuality is undermined.

Triple-Loop Learning

When we finally get what is meant by "learning enterprise" it alters how we intersect. In his confessional *Practices for Recovering Knowers*,[4] Brian Hinken joins servant leadership and *epistemic humility* in the term *Triple-Loop Learning*. Let's explore the three loops.

Unilateral Control—Changing Our Doing—*Single-Loop Learning*

Unilateral control is the paradigm of self-centered ambition. It animates the behavior of knowers.

We demand an outcome. We devise tactics on assumptions what works, why. If it doesn't we suppose that this time calls for a different one of our gems. We cycle through the old playbook until we hit on one that works. Bias traps us in an infinite loop.

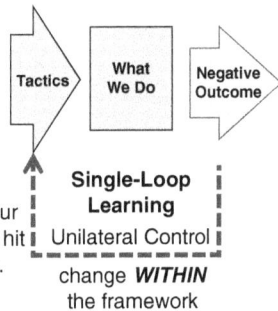

Tactics > What We Do > Negative Outcome

Single-Loop Learning
Unilateral Control
change **WITHIN** the framework

On flawed assumptions, our tactics become part of the problem. This is **change *within* the framework**. It traces back to the knower's failure to join our fractional knowledge with others', to extend.

Mutual Learning—*Changing Our Thinking*—***Double-Loop Learning***[5]

Knower's *hubris* produces single-loop action but no information.

**Faulty Assumptions
seed Misguided Tactics
yield Negative Outcomes**

Gaps appear where we need to align tactical presumption to reality. Tactics misalign to strategy. Periodically, we review Δ expected -vs -actual outcomes of our tactics. Is *how* we are going about it why we don't achieve as expected? On structured questioning, Double-Loop Learning produces **action** *and* **information.**

| Core Values & Assumptions | Tactics | What We Do | Negative Outcome |

Double-Loop Learning
Mutual Learning
change the
FRAMEWORK

Single-Loop Learning
Unilateral Control
change **WITHIN**
the framework

Revising Obsolete Assumptions:
1. Why do I really want this result?
2. What made me think prior tactics would work ?
Ideas have consequences.

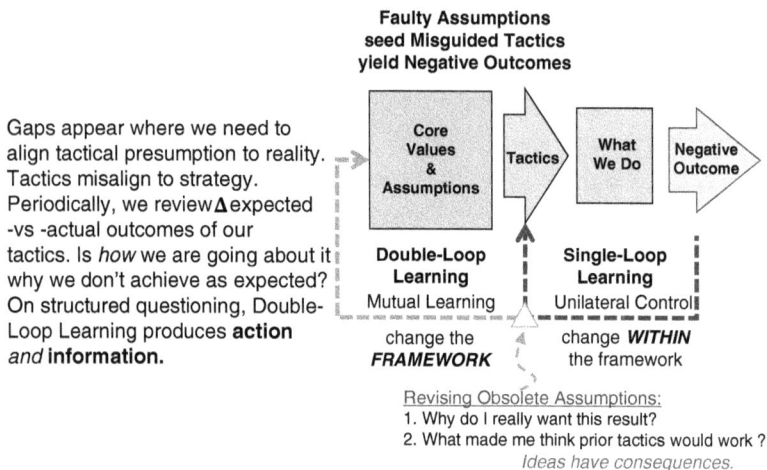

Now we are getting somewhere, but we're not quite done yet.

Triple-Loop Learning—Changing Our Being—Change in the Framer

Telos	the overarching purpose - meta-agenda.
Strategy	a structured plan to bring about a desired future – what we aim to become (as enterprise, or as persons).
Strategy Deployment	an adaptive design, a PDCA Try, to close a gap Δ in means
(hoshin kanri)	needed for advance from current to desired next stage.

In complexity, strategies easily fail to account for the *means* to realistically attain expectations. The framer's design may be the gap:

- Failure to supply a needed *capacity*
- Failure to supply a needed *capability*
- Directed *compass heading* is bent from True North

Or, framers' fallibility may be the gap. Our guides need to reset their *capacity*, *capability*, and *compass*, to remain effective in framing and executing strategy. An especially notorious failure mode is using strategy as a prop to affirm the framer's *self*-image or to signal our virtues. For all, the diverted resources would be better spent in True North inquiry.

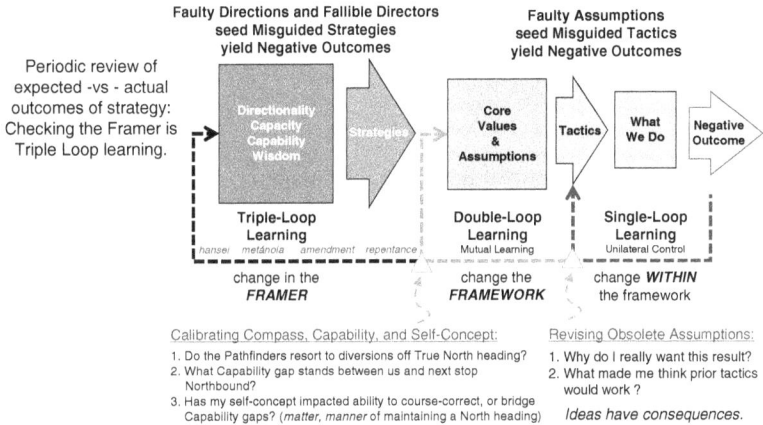

This Third Loop is what *The Toyota Way*[6] recommends in Principle 14 as *hansei*.

Hansei

Japanese parents use *hansei* in the discipline (or response to an achievement) of their children. It guides moving on from here to "next". *Hansei* is a structured pause, sequester, to deliberate on cause. It appeals to a person's sense of direction. The learner brings back a plan to prevent recurrence of the regrettable. Or they speak to how to translate victory lessons into further gains.

A French farmer may recognize this as *amendement*—preparation of fields toward a future produce. Some use this metaphor in the discipline of their loved ones. This expression is deeply embedded in English: Where discipline is constructive, when we send a loved one off to reflect after an episode, we ask them to bring back a plan for how they will *make amends*.

Framers of the *Constitution* chose *amendment* to word-paint how to adaptively treat gaps in their plan for a nation. They enshrined *amendment* as a revered instance of Leader Standard Work: Divided neighbors can revisit, sort out, and co-adapt forward toward True North.

The Greeks called this *metánoia*—an image of 180° turnabout of direction, of the will. *Hansei* has its modern English equivalent—*repentance*. Frankly, it is unpopular.

Self-evaluation is very personal. It impacts public image. Rivals can manipulate admissions to further competing agendas at the expense of our honesty. Fools interpret meekness as weakness, though it is power under control. Naturally, there is hesitation on the topic. Nobody has room for presumption.

Amendment not just of impersonal framework, but personally in the framer, is of great value in learning then leading. It fuels sustaining and radically reforms cooperation that had gotten bent along the way.

Leader Standard Work

Leader Standard Work (LSW) brings triple-loop learners around to the intersections that are supposed to be joining us in extended order. It exploits tactics of structure and cadence, across the leader's span of contribution and control:

- For leader time management efficiency
- For transmission, storage, communication of information at the intersections
    - Resource attainment—escalation, coordination
    - Compliance and containment
    - Meta-agenda—*telos*

Triple-loop thinking requires unfiltered feedback in a loop, not one-way directives. LSW goes out to pull it. It is a check on whether the hypotheses of strategy and tactics actually work. In LSW the leader cycles through the span of responsibility on structured cadence. Providers serve users—not the other way around. We proactively go assess the state of service we are supposed to have delivered.

This circuit is a PDCA loop, an informational trap-line. Provider (trapper) will *go-see* what got caught on the expectations of SCQDP. Providers go confirm directly, with the questions of the triple loop in mind:

- What is actual versus expected outcome of tactics, and underlying strategy?
- What needed resources for SCQDP are lacking punctually, on the spot?
- Do barriers hinder those we serve, from attaining what was expected?

Countermeasure to Incommensurable Paradigms That Fracture Extended Order

Leader Standard Work is like an avalanche cannon. Alpine villages concuss the hills around on a cadence. It is better to set off attenuated series of daily little cascades all winter, than to cower in fear of a Big One that builds up enough to bury us for eternity.

LSW continually chips away at partial information and unreliable supposition. It goes out to **remove the insulation between elites and value-adding laity.** It is real-time reconciliation to the realities that beset the *gemba*. LSW is the ongoing effort to *falsify* standard, using the battering ram of reality.

It is muscular mutuality, *amendment* on steroids. It freshly signals emerging need for adaptation of specialization between leadership, services, and front-liners. Viewing ourselves rightly is the key to rightly viewing others. This is at the heart of breakthrough at the enterprise level.

Considering How to Learn

Complexity creates great need for effective organizational instruction. Education and industry have been waging costly struggles through vogues and disputes over methods. There are many approaches to teaching and learning—didactic, heuristic, dialectic, parabolic, Socratic, and so on. The Socratic method is the one that has risen to recent emphasis in OpEx.

Socratic runs deep in **TWI** *Job Instruction*, which awakened U.S. industries in the 1940s, then rebooted Japan. *If student hasn't learned, teacher hasn't taught.* Rother and Liker's generational works have rekindled interest (*Toyota Way*, *Toyota Kata*). These come as correctives to a century of didactic excess in perfecting ambitions of knowers, at the expense of mutual learning that could have bonded shareholders and value-adders.

Didactic Instruction

Didactic transmits data or method from a discoverer (authority) to learners not-yet in mastery of it. It brings hearers current on stored knowledge. This aids them in going forth to their own figuring-out. So far, so good.

Knowers show little patience for normals exploring their own questions for themselves. *Scientific Management* overextended didactic beyond just giving a head-start with data. It morphed into indoctrination— prescribing approved questions and aims. Knowers of course are the ones who get to say. Didactics jumped the shark. Read Frederick Taylor on *Scientific Management* to see how it all plays out for workers and experts:

> The burden of gathering together all of the traditional knowledge which in the past has been possessed by the workmen and then of classifying, tabulating, and reducing this knowledge to rules, laws, formula . . . must . . . be done by management in accordance with the law of science.[7]

One can see why didactic instruction now is met with suspicion. Effort is being made to revitalize mutual learning. Still, didactic instruction properly centered, is irreplaceable in equipping learners to effectively do inquiry.

For example, learning to read is useful in shaping pupils into inquirers. First one must know an alphabet. English has 26 base characters— not 21, not 37—and there is no point in pupils voting on it. To begin, the 26 are transmitted didactically to aspiring readers. Language formation is emergent.[8] *Beowulf,* the *King James Bible,* and *On a Louse* cited above, all show this. Learners amend language, because it can always be made to serve better. Persons not didactically taught an alphabet would struggle to contribute to evolving a language. Emojis and extended characters come, at later stages of mixed inquiry and use.

The world's stock of stored knowledge grows exponentially. Learners require a great deal of didactic instruction to even grasp current state in complex enterprise. Rather than corporate witch hunts to purge didactic instruction, learning is better-served undoing the past misuses. *Those who don't learn from the past are condemned to repeat it.*

Socratic

Socratic coaching is not communication of data. It is not advice on the circumstances: It transmits *stored* knowledge—the knowledge of how to form great questions, to effectively sort out answers.

As Juran put it, **data only answer the questions that got asked**.[9] Rather than giving answers, like mother birds furnish babies their prey, a Socratic coach poses chains of questions. These questions are designed to guide steps by which learners learn to form the right questions to then unravel their own inquiry.

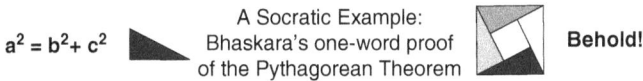

$$a^2 = b^2 + c^2$$

A Socratic Example:
Bhaskara's one-word proof
of the Pythagorean Theorem

Behold!

In a way Socratics are answerers of questions with questions. Asking, to set off investigation, exposes not just "what" but "how" to learn. It is a nice contrast to paternalistic prescription that knowers have long inflicted on the rest.

Balance is in order: Issuing torrents of interrogation at every simple encounter wears out learners. Posturing Socratics are just as paternalistic as any über-didactic scold. Socrates was called *the gadfly of Athens*.[10] He did not much bend to the culture. His people made him drink hemlock and die. Ever-indirect replies to questioners with only more questions may have hastened his demise. For learning how to learn, didactic instruction will not alone suffice. Nor will Socratic alone. Good leaders learn to choose the right tool for each learning situation.

A theme of this book is *ad fontes*—to the sources: *Open Society and Its Enemies* (Popper) is a good source on restoring reason and science in teaching and leading. Vol. 1, Chapter 7 contrasts Socrates' insistence on inquiry, against Plato's urging that teaching and leading be exclusive and autocratic. Hayek's *Counter-Revolution of Science* is another good source on righting the abuses of reason, rescuing the sciences from authoritarian hijack. As Socrates famously put it,

Whatever authority I may have rests solely upon my knowing how little I know.[11]

These sources are heavy but worthy. They focus on governance. In this book, we stick to our own knitting: parallels for operations in enterprise. Popper and Hayek contributed respectful, deep thought. Current-day management debates have deep, historic roots.

CHAPTER 13

Breakthrough Knowing
What We Don't Know

Man is no Aristotelian god contemplating all existence at one glance.
—Walter Lippmann

It is only our profound and comprehensive ignorance of the nature of culture that makes it possible for us to believe that we direct and control it.[1]
—L.A. White

PDCA: The Improvement *Kata*

Science is grassroots use of *induction* to penetrate our threshold of knowledge.[2] It starts off realistic but challenging—with an attempted step toward True North that we do not yet know how to do. In iterative tries we learn a path from current- to target-condition:

Plan.	Lay out a rearrangement we believe can bump the system to a desired outcome.
	Stake a claim: *Doing **X** should move the needle to **Y**.* Design a try, so that if our idea of cause and effect is incomplete, it will get *falsified* by the conditions it is exposed to.
Do it.	Try may be the better word for this iterative investigative step. Follow through.
Check.	If outcome is not as predicted . . .
Adjust.	Persist in forward-running loops until we learn how to get to **Y** and hold it.

Falsification

Our attempt to demonstrate cause and effect may have been wrong as to cause but be right on cure, or right on cause, but wrong as to the cure. There may be hidden conditionals—only partially right. Due to unexpected factors, **X** doesn't yield **Y** every time like we said it would. The outcome may go further, or not as far as predicted. Somehow, explanation is incomplete on the effect we set out to observably cause. It is a fallacy to view falsified tries as failures. Falsification outs the suspects we hadn't known about when we planned the trial. Falsification—not having been entirely right after all—forces us to choose: evasion, or learning:

- We could take a knower's stance about variation and admission of what we don't kno*w*: Short term, this is the easier path. Many companies work hard to avoid, discipline, legislate away, or try to design out not being right in the hypotheses we test. We are pressed to make things quit varying. On appraisals, money talks and pep slogans walk.
- Or, we can take the learner's posture: Appreciate that falsification has outed a stealth factor. But for our trial, that factor would have been left to bite us later. Now we can adjust our plans, and bend this additional factor to our aims, too.

This paradigm of falsification and variability embraces the investment aspect of learning: *Problems Are Treasures*. Deviation does carry costs. No doubt, repeatability is a relief. Pressing operations toward zero variability and some "ideal" of mastery sounds nice. It's a good thing that we don't always get what we want.

Some amount of variability in a complex system serves important uses. Aversion to all variation devolves from passive neglect into active suppression of adaptability. It begs a visit from the **Black Swan**. Those who push too many *sigmas* down the road of eliminating all variation render their systems **fragile**. *Bifurcation* is a well-known feature, not an unforeseeable bug. It can be a certified witch when it (surely) visits. See Nassim Taleb's *Antifragile*.

Variation costs. But knee-jerk extermination of all variability is worse. The fathers of information science crafted a clever balance that enlightens why we call problems *treasures*.

Claude Shannon

Popular notions of "planning" increasingly revolve around acquisition of big data whose aim is to know (see) exhaustively all variations in a system. Knowing all deviations is prized because it is presumed to equate to eventual power to eliminate them all. The assumption is that zero variation would be a good thing. In our struggles with change, that does sound nice.

The establishment (cognitive) paradigm of "planning" is to know (eliminate) the unknowns between us and complete control. Shannon made a game-changing observation: **Information is ability to distinguish reliably among alternative possible meanings**. It is signal lifted out of noise. What we need is to inform variation, not necessarily eliminate it all.

Complex systems emit trainloads of data. More data do not (necessarily) equal more information, and can make for less. We left constants, "given," and equilibrium behind in the lecture hall. In complexity, planners are never going to *know* in a godlike way.

In the "hard" sciences, the observable is the key to cause. But in complexity and social science, often what we *do not know* (hard or impossible to clinically observe) holds the key to cause. Shannon did an end-run on diminishing marginal returns of eliminating all *unknowns*. He pivoted focus onto probability—how best to reason in presence of uncertainty. He shifted aim from knowing to adaptive learning. Even falsified predictions fuel next steps.

To sift guidance out of the conflicting and unclear, we hedge tries on *probably* right, often enough to offset some misses. Probability progressively walks us to a payoff.

The **amount of surprise in a message reflects how much information it contains**. Surprise in a message is *Shannon's entropy*. Not all messages are alike. Surprises teach us more: A mailbox flag, doorbell, or *andon* light has two possible messages—On/Off. Off is the default.

There is not much information in a doorbell that is silent. Most of the time it is this way. So, exceptions and problems are treasures. They are information-rich.

R.V.L. Hartley

Hartley added his own profound simplicity about information:

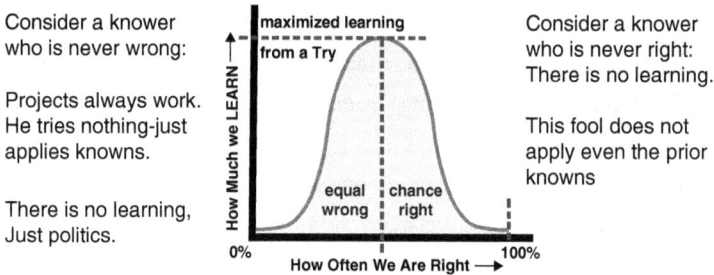

Consider a knower who is never wrong:

Projects always work. He tries nothing-just applies knowns.

There is no learning, Just politics.

Consider a knower who is never right: There is no learning.

This fool does not apply even the prior knowns

Learning gained in a Try is maximized at equal chance of being wrong

Hoisting the Jolly Roger, a lit *andon*, empty *kanban*, the ringing doorbell—these are uncommon. They contain much news. They inform a provider—unambiguously—of who, how, and when they need to act. When the hypothesis behind our big idea gets falsified in a trial, it comes as a surprise—*it contains much information (Shannon's entropy) to fuel our next steps.*

When we experiment, being wrong comes at a cost. Had we been right, we would be a step closer to target condition. Naturally we want ideas to work. But to accelerate discovery we have to admit an increase in rate of being wrong. There is no virtue in being wrong for wrong's sake. For sake of discovery, how can an organization justify an increase in its experiments turning out "wrong"—say, up to half the time?

Mitigating the Increased Rate of Unsuccessful Tries

1. **Privilege Swarms of Rapid, Reversible Little Tries**
   Quit treating discovery as cancer trials or international missions to Neptune. Swinging for the fences every at-bat impedes learning.

Celebrate grand slams that do come, but aim at simple on-base percentage, where most scoring comes from.

Bobby White recounts the time his coach benched a guy for hitting a home run. It undermined the larger scheme—pitch count. The coach was Cy Young Award winner Denny McClain. As he put it, *Home Runs are rally killers.* Mega-projects breed solutions "*too big to fail*". Being wrong becomes impermissible. Life-or-death stakes distort what learners will try. It corrupts feedback—*slay the bearer of bad news.* It hogs the oxygen, suffocating many respectable gains we might have done by now in its place.

Rapid, reversible tries are preferred. Learn what there is, then worst case, put things back as they were. Move forward on incremented information sum.

2. **Oblige Learners to Mine This "Failure": Inform the Next Try**
Well-designed inquiry outs hidden conditionals. It lifts factors out of noise, increasing the surprise at their appearance. A good illustration is the game "Twenty Questions." In search of a needle in a haystack, failures narrow down the stack. Some falsifications tell us more than confirmations would.

The price of predicting "wrong" is that the learner needs to answer: *What did this experience suggest for a next try?* Improvement at its best, means every person—every process—a little bit every day.

Lean Is Applied Information Science

Lean improves systems by treating variation: That doesn't always mean reducing it. Some variation needs to be put to work, to propel opportunistic value creation. There is great diversity of kinds of lean deliverables (*kanban, andon, Takt,* operator balance, Leader Standard Work, etc.). But all trace to a common thread—lean practices are information devices:

- Lean practices emit a real-time signal, at breaches in the flow of value.
- Lean arranges stakeholders into *kata* most favorable to the re-formation of order.

○ It informs unambiguous response in the face of alternative ways to rejoin efforts.

○ It informs effectual division of labor with mutuality.

○ It informs containment and restored flow.

○ It resets troubled operations in a way that informs underlying problem-solving.

Lean works by increasing efficiency of messaging. It reduces uncertainty among alternative interpretations. Its boosts signal-to-noise ratio in forming, sending, receiving, and storage of information. It assembles partial knowledges in a sum that boosts surprise content. In contributing their fragment each actor is returned the information sum, from across the extended order. It helps distinguish our best order-forming response in context, toward the strategy.

Perspective and Scale on The Knowledge Problem

Operational revolutions have left us great creeds for learning. Toyota Way's **14 Principles** is chief. Deming's **14 Points** were influential. All strike a common chord: A crying need for *constancy of purpose* in face of the knowledge problem. Deming opens with it. It is the coda of Liker's *Toyota Way*: *"Learning Organization Is a Long-Term Journey."*

Our own work feels historic, when we look back on how long we toiled. Ours feels informed, by so much investigation over nights and years. We recall vast distances from start to here. This is not to diminish or call us puny. Celebrate achievement, but seek perspective.

It is irrelevant, how big I am (or not) relative to neighbors—that is the wrong standard. Any one's contribution is dwarfed by the sum of knowledge and time to build a complexity. Meta-agenda requires an objective yardstick, the system sum.

Leonard Reed illustrates in his storybook *I, Pencil*:

I, Pencil, simple though I appear to be, merit your wonder and awe . . . not a single person on the face of this earth knows how to make me. . . . Not much meets the eye . . . wood, lacquer, the printed labeling, graphite lead, a bit of metal, and an eraser.

There isn't a single person in all these millions, including the president of the pencil company, who contributes more than a tiny, infinitesimal bit of know-how.

The graphite is mined in Ceylon. Consider these miners and . . . their many tools and the makers of the paper sacks in which the graphite is shipped . . . the string that ties the sacks and those who put them aboard ships and those who make the ships. Even the lighthouse keepers along the way assisted in my birth—and the harbor pilots.

The graphite is mixed with clay from Mississippi . . . ammonium hydroxide is used in the refining process. Then wetting agents are added . . . animal fats chemically reacted with sulfuric acid. After passing through numerous machines . . . finally appears . . . as from a sausage grinder—cut to size, dried, and baked for several hours . . . leads are then treated with a hot mixture which includes candelilla wax from Mexico, paraffin wax.

From the standpoint of know-how the only difference between the miner of graphite in Ceylon and the logger in Oregon is in the type of know-how. Neither the miner nor the logger can be dispensed with, any more than can the chemist at the factory or the worker in the oil field—paraffin being a by-product of petroleum. . . . I, Pencil, am a complex combination of miracles: a tree, zinc, copper, graphite, and so on.

An even more extraordinary miracle has been added: the configuration of creative human energies—millions of tiny know-hows configurating naturally and spontaneously . . . in the absence of any human masterminding!

Since only God can make a tree, I insist that only God could make me. Man can no more direct these millions of know-hows to bring me into being than he can put molecules together to create a tree.[3]

The economist Vilfredo Pareto recognized the knowledge problem, mathematically:

of 100 persons and 700 commodities there will be 70,699 conditions (actually a great number of circumstances which we have so far neglected will still increase that number); We shall, therefore, have to solve a system of 70,699 equations.[4]

Complex enterprise involves many more than 100 persons. The things we trade off number many more than 700. Mises laid out this enormity, in all its partial differential glory.

If one really could know all these equations, the only means to solve them which is available to human powers is to observe the practical solution given by the market.[5]

It works wonders of perspective to lay my own learning and time, against the scale of additional contributors who are just as vital as *moi*. Each of them, too, invested time and knowledge, a vast system-wide sum, for our complexity to have extended this far. My (vital) piece pales in comparison to the vast scope of moving a complexity from current-state any distance at all toward True North.

When we reflect how much knowledge possessed by other people is an essential condition for the pursuit of our individual aims, the magnitude of our ignorance of the circumstances on which the results of our action depend appears simply staggering.[6]

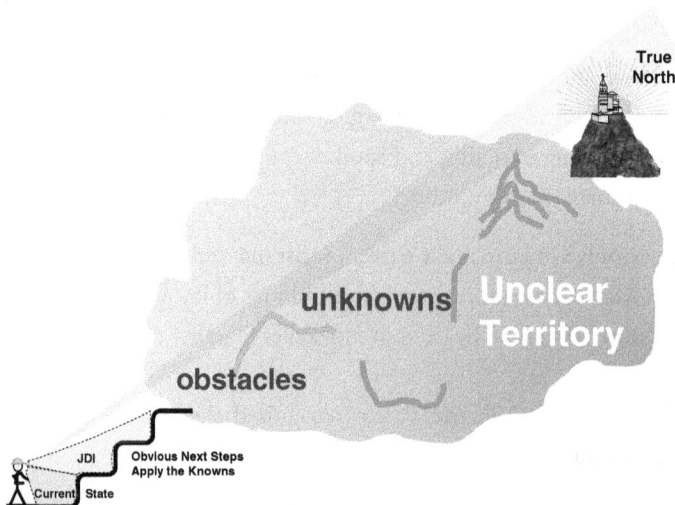

Accurate scaling of the dimensions of 'me' is foundational to servant leadership.

What Kind of *Gemba* Boards Actually Work?

In *The Creative Powers of a Free Civilization*[7] Hayek unpacks why Managing for Daily Improvement boards (MDI), *kata* storyboards, and exception management methods work. Ones that work are not marquees or billboards for what we did and know. *Ones that work crystallize what we* don't *know, but ought to.*

Displays that matter suppose that leaders and services don't come out to hold court. Seeking feedback, they come to enhance flow of value-add at *gemba. Signals that matter arise in consequence of running, not ruling.* Proper boards carry signals laden with surprise. Wise customers proactively inform suppliers. It is in their enlightened, mutual interest to do so.

MDI makes Standard Work doable for a busy leader struggling to span a broad stretch of control. In under a minute she can discern need-to-know and need-to-share, without pulling the worker out-of-cycle. If a distillation of *don't know* is not waiting, she comes to check, only to squander her time gathering Δ. It leaves little bandwidth to then do anything about it.

Focus on What We Don't Know

Part 3 offers measures to sustain improvement. The key to this chapter is to shift our gaze from what we *do* know, to act more effectively in light of that greater sum of what we *don't.*

> Civilization begins when the individual in pursuit of his ends can make use of more knowledge than he has himself acquired and when he can transcend the boundaries of his ignorance by profiting from knowledge he himself does not possess.[8]

Limits of the Scientific Method

In natural science, to investigate with objectivity is to isolate how a thing works, scrupulously independent of anything the actors think or wish. It centers on what we know. We equate knowing with observability, reproducing it so everyone can see it empirically.

Social sciences and complexity pose a mostly different problem. What people think *is* almost entirely what drives how they interact—whether cooperation will extend, or fracture. Manner of interaction is the formal cause, and behavioral shifts the pacemaker. These are more *un*-seen than seen. Math doesn't readily depict these. Constructing falsifiable, reproducible hypotheses can be exceedingly difficult in this domain.

Just because a complexity can fit equations to its past macro track, it is not the same thing as the ability to make falsifiable, non-obvious, specific predictions. Describing the past is not being *scientific*. Geologists could not have stood by any of the Three Rivers when the continent was young and said where the Steelers would someday play, at their confluence today.

> When we reflect how much knowledge possessed by other people is an essential condition for the pursuit of our individual aims, the magnitude of our ignorance of the circumstances on which the results of our action depend appears simply staggering.[9]

We speak of "organizational learning," but a team is not a sentient being. Persons are the possessors of knowing—each a fragment. The combined sum exists nowhere as a whole.

> The great problem is how we can all profit from this knowledge, which exists only dispersed as the separate, partial, and sometimes conflicting beliefs of all men.[10]

Division of Knowledge

Under specialization and comparative advantage, we saw why division of labor is compelling to groups hoping to improve. But it contains seeds of its own undoing. Division of labor means **division of knowledge.** Sustaining means to divide knowledge without dividing the group that hold it. It means staying subscribed to abstract, rule-connected mutuality through the changes.

As we divide labor we entrust the circumstances of time and place to increasingly many others down the stream. The sum of knowledge grows. The fraction of that sum that any one of us holds becomes vanishingly small in modern complexity.

At every actor, countless little changes arise that set off iterative little adjustments. These affect peers at interfaces, cascading adjustment to the adjustment, counters and pushback, adjustment to adjustment's adjustment, on down a value stream. A bump gradually resolves by collaborative rearrangement across system, toward a new "equilibrium." A complex enterprise likely never arrives at equilibrium before the next cascade.

As this runs, circumstantial knowledge grows at each *gemba*. Fraction of total knowledge held by any one is small. It grows smaller as complexity extends. For this to work, necessitates:

> that each individual be able to act on his particular knowledge . . . at least so far as it refers to some particular circumstances, and that he be able to use his individual skills and opportunities within the limits.[11]

This manner of trust is not instinctive; it is earned and learned, harder as complexity extends.

> Collective judgement of new ideas is so often wrong that . . . progress depends on individuals being free to back their own judgement despite collective disapproval.[12]

Improvement in every person-process-day is core to sustaining. Recombinance extends this further still, as we will see in a later chapter.

> The chief characteristic of the command hierarchy . . . is not knowledge but ignorance. Consider that any one person can only know a fraction of what is going on. . . . Much of what that person knows or believes will be false rather than true.

> At any given time, vastly more is not known than is known, either by one person in a command chain or by all the organization. It seems possible then, that in organizing ourselves into a hierarchy of authority for the purpose of increasing efficiency, we may really be institutionalizing ignorance.

> **While making better use of what the few know, we are making sure that the great majority are prevented from exploring the dark areas beyond our knowledge.**[13]

CHAPTER 14

Leveling the Cycle

You win championships when the stands are empty.

—Dabo Swinney

Like Saturn, revolution devours its children.

—Jacques Mallet du Pan

Rich and poor differ greatly in outlook of what to do about sustenance. Seen from the street, it has a lot to do with learning and breakthrough. Then prosperity softens muscular ideals about change. Seen from the penthouse, sustaining looks like maintaining the sweet *status quo*. Thoughts of what we need turn increasingly to control (hold on), becoming less about breakthrough (move on).

It decomposes sustainment, to look to improvement as a cyclical reaction, something for when issues mount up to intolerable. Where change is a rollercoaster, we invest the dimensions of a next crisis, in proportion to the fall-off we allow from peak discovery to depth of incuriosity.

Constants aren't, and variables don't. Standards hold controls static, while issues they were put there to contain, mutate. Know-how grows a *reality gap*. It is wise to exploit variability continually, to refresh the revelation and the investigation of the gaps in how we try to use cause and effect.

Simplistic notions of control as stamping out all variability, unwittingly smother the learning aspect of change. Decline is a bad sort of change. But breakthrough is a type of change, too. Putting it off, discovering in surges, is a truly bad idea. Pauses work like capacitors: Learning in boom-and-bust cycles allows anomaly to store up to crisis levels. As Kuhn elaborated, at some limit crisis discharges revolution. Revolution is a cruel form of change. Renaissance and Reformation are much kinder.

The Evil Triplets: Muda, Mura, Muri

A hallmark of the Toyota Production System (TPS) is "*Learning to See*" what stands between us and True North. Lean's vision is binary: we categorize endeavors as either value-adding or value-subtracting. Value-subtraction is further subdivided into: *Muda, mura,* and *muri.*

Muda is **waste** of effort and treasure; futility, vanity.

Mura is **unevenness** of flow between connected processes.

Muri is **overburden** of system components.

Muda

This most tangible aspect of loss subdivides into a universal, actionable "Eight Wastes": Transport, improper inventory, excess motion, human talent underemployed, waiting, overproduction, overprocessing, and defects.

These are the easily seen losses. They receive a lot of superficial publicity. We see these at points of *symptom*. Points of cause often lie elsewhere. Hunting *muda* yields mostly point improvement. System thinking, to improve and sustain at enterprise-level, requires that we also address the two lesser-known nonvalue siblings.

Mura *and* Muri

Unevenness and overburden are not wastes per se: They are *disease markers* on its points of cause, like PSA marks prostate cancer, and hemoglobins mark diabetes. *Mura* and *muri* are not-flow behaviors—markers of underlying loss inherent in how we have chosen to operate:

Unevenness signals wasteful *manner of connection* at an intersection.

Overburden signals wasteful *allocation of share* at a step in a value chain.

We don't see the wind, but moving leaves tell us it is blowing. Leaves are to wind as not-flow is to value-subtraction. Unevenness and overburden mark the lairs of that which squanders effort and treasure.

Unevenness and overburden in the discovery process counter sustainment, by amplifying the demands and disruptions of the anomaly-revolution cycle. We invest the dimensions of a next crisis, in proportion to the let-up we permit, from peak discovery to depth of incuriosity.

There's a word for leaders who approve *burning platforms*—arsonists. It is not the perfecting of crisis drivers, but rather the taming of them, that sets us on the path to sustain. Revolutionary spasms—unevenness and overburden—spawn charlatans, caste systems, Stalins, regret, and eventually revolution when reality overtakes narrative. Evolution—reformation—is a cheaper, kinder way to transform, than is revolution.

Life Is a Batch and Then You Die

Flow beats batching. You can swallow whole peas one after another. You won't enjoy trying it with apples. Getting good at sustaining means taming the excesses of breakthrough's boom-and-bust cycles. Batching behavior drives the size of anomaly we end up having to swallow.

Status \stā-təs\   noun, a static place where we have arrived.

Sustain \sə-'stān\   verb, a dynamic of *vectoring* toward True North.

Sustain means holding *velocity* and *heading*, not just holding place. Leveling the *rate* of improvement is the idea.

Flow where you can. Pull where you must. Never Push.

A knower's batch-and-queue approach to discovery amplifies boom-and-bust. Learners see there is need to detect lulls from the start, and rein in little speed and course deviations without oversteering. This chapter and the next lay out the "hows," along three main lines:

- Level the learning cycles.
- Balance exploration with exploitation (normal operation)
  - In parallel, rather than the batchiness of series. Both—not either/or.
- Augment exploration—cleverly milk some of it out of routine operations.

Leveled Learning Cycles

Crisis breeds where **providers get insulated from realities of users** accountable to deliver on our rules and provisions. *Shear a sheep many times, but you can skin him only once.*

To see knowledge as partial and dispersed causes us to seek and link mutual learning. It pulls us to the gaps where strategy, tactics, rules, and resourcing fall short on enabling to deliver. Group dynamics begin to look like cadenced triple-loop inquiry at *gemba*—**Standard Work**.

It is easy to lose sight of the mutuality proposition that led up to specialization. Thus, we ask specialists and providers to practice the triple-loop *kata*. It's not just for bosses. Influencers of rival factions, those guiding hiring and advancement, and resource allocators, have double the need to practice the triple loop.

If gaps are let go too far, rival explanations diverge to irreconcilable. Partisans get conditioned to a point that they are no longer able to process what *"others"* even mean if they try to explain. The sides become *hearing but not understanding, seeing but not perceiving.*

Frequency Unlocks Amplitude

Little, frequent inquiries make space to work a sort of rolling consensus: Actively outing where we disagree. Consensus facilitation is not to hold court and pick who's first among rivals, not to bend every knee to a common aim, but to jointly devise testing of differences and next steps.

Leveled Countermeasuring Cycles

A natural response to the above is to surge Leader Standard Work across the house. Knowledge is fragmentary. We wildly underestimate how many gaps there are. This brings us to the number-one reason that lean initiatives crater: We have fundamentally mistaken what lean is. Lean is the most efficient way ever devised to *expose* gaps. Left there, exposing *solves* nothing.

Drones deploy tools because they heard that "Toyota does it", or, because corporate has pronounced it to be "Standard." The lean practices then proceed to expose so much that it overwhelms all capacity to resolve. It shuts down flow.

Then the laity step in and save us from ourselves—they quit the system. The experts left them no choice. We failed to resolve the first several-hundred issues they brought. They check out, to go keep producing, while "experts" deliberate. Launching what will bust open all our gaps, without resourcing to address them, is weapons-grade naiveté. What begins as unpreparedness ends in mean, not lean, enterprise. *Count the cost.*

Passive decline may be preferable to oblivious release of every issue we ever locked up (pacified) with an excess of inventory, capacity, and leadtime.

We must pre-stage the capacity to triage and resolve real-time, against the issues jailbreak certain to accompany Lean launch.

Y'all skin this one while I go find the next.

OpEx

Undertake the lean effort where leadership has provisioned to resolve what is exposed, by structured PDCA, in service to those about to get stirred. As Soichiro Honda put it, *Action without philosophy is a lethal weapon. Philosophy without action is worthless.*

Where mutuality lives, frequent little checks yield swarms of competing, even contradictory, reversible countermeasures. Standard Work is a noisy *discovery process*. Little gaps don't conceive the big anomaly. Rolling consensus doesn't carry anomaly full-term to crisis. Crisis doesn't birth revolution unless a critical mass let it go there. With a will, brewing crises can find a glide path to calmer reformations.

Leader Standard Work + MDI + structured PDCA response is the action combo that clears off what insulates providers from the realities users face. LSW is the renewal of mutuality.

Balancing Exploration with Exploitation

The breakthrough cycle involves two fundamental kinds of activity: exploration and exploitation. Exploitation is normal operations—the reaping of what we sow and what we know. Exploration is like a search for the high ground. We are looking (exploring) for a place to securely build up what matters (exploit) and improve from there. Wherever we choose to settle down (standard) and exploit, variability inevitably comes to pay us a visit.

Pure Exploration Is a Novelty Trap

Cultures have phases when new is categorically assumed just better.

Welfare is diminished if we spend the treasury on the kind of discovery that never settles in to pay back in results.

Unexploited novelty, for its own sake, is value-subtracting.

Pure Exploitation Is a Competency Trap

"Pragmatism" runs to impatience. If we settle too fast, we leave money on the table, and build up undue exposure to complex risk.

Settling on a Flood Zone

We settle on first hilltop, a local suboptimum. We don't press on to global peak.

ROI does kick in fast where we settle quickly.

By flood season, it may not seem so pragmatic after all.

Settling at the Water's Edge

Life sets up fast at water's edge. Settle too early in the wrong spot, and the tides may go out and strand us.

Tidal pools are pragmatic for sea birds. For early adopter crabs and fish, not so much.

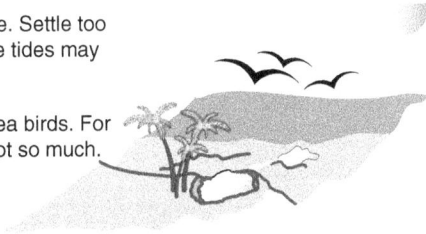

A sloppy, imprecise paradigm of how they relate pits value-adding against value-aid in a tug-of-war. This shapes work into needless, batchy lurches back and forth. Sustainment requires clarity, connected balance not opposition, and continuity of both as an integral part of normal operations.

Exploration is Value-Aiding	Exploitation is Value-Adding
Out-of-cycle service operation.	In-cycle routine operation.
Discovery process, spends treasury to extend know-how in use of cause-effect to improve advantage	Apply stored know-how on cause-effect, exploiting knowledge of circumstance, to deliver value into the treasury.
Both are needed in balance, to extend order - today and tomorrow - sustain.	

Value-Subtraction[1]

For "value-add" we hear many fuzzy examples in place of definition. Steven Kates helps, with a term *"value-subtraction."* A treasury contains *value—the ability to produce its members' means of living*—utility.

A silo of corn can seed and produce hundreds more siloes full. Or it can be drawn down to make a load of cornbread for the hungry—once. Any grain eaten is a one-and-done, no longer available to yield ears full. Consumption (terminal, one-time use) trades away some amount of our capacity to produce. Most things produced in complex enterprise are value-subtracting:

> Using stock to make intermediate goods draws down the silo: It *transforms* resources (with loss), but adds nothing back into treasury. This may one day contribute to value, but has not yet. Transforming treasure into WIP assigns identity, barring it from alternatives it might have served, if circumstance shifts on us. This loss of optionality is value-subtracting.
>
> Until we convert goods to a customer and net a tangible profit, WIP value-subtracts. This is not how balance sheets present WIP, but it is how to see it economically. Ideas have consequences. Complex methods require WIP, toward eventual *presumably* greater ends. But it is *value-subtracting*, unless and until actual profit is consummated.

Repair, upkeep, meals, entertainment, and consumer goods are *consumption*. These eat seed corn. They put nothing back into the silo toward a next crop. A dollar spent on these is forever gone to future use. Many of these are necessary, some noble. But, all said, they subtract value, as seen from the silo. Everyone's standard of living (ability to produce) goes up when we devise how to do less of things like repair without compromising the integrity of the operation.

Value-subtraction does not mean zero value was produced

Value-subtraction means this put less value back in than it drew out for use. Net potential for thriving after today, got drawn down, not added to. As Bastiat told in his parable of broken windows,[2] we cannot sustain by promoting loss-making projects. Living standard increases only by elevating the fraction and kind of activity that returns more into treasury than it draws.

Sustaining means getting better at consummating intermediate value-aiding effort into end-goods, for net gain to silo. This is the lean sense of "value-add." Steven Covey called it a *production–production capability* dilemma.[3]

To exploit, we privilege value-add for flow at the pull of demand. All the while, value-aid is clearly delineated, subordinated, leveled, but never suffocated. Without value-aid we can't add value for long. If value-aid goes unconsummated or gets prioritized over value-add, it drives boom-and-bust, cyclic batching.

"Exploration and Exploitation in Organizational Learning"[4]

This work by James March is a foundational source for leveling. Organizational learning is an anthropomorphism, like "carbon footprint." Teams don't learn—persons do. We advance group know-how where we efficiently join it. March gives pointers how to steadily draw lessons out of the variations of mute operations. It is all to do with how we hire and develop. Many companies proclaim, *employees are our greatest asset*. Then, this should be of great interest.

The Learning Curve

Extending order divides labor, thus knowledge. What we must know to operate grows in time and division of labor/knowledge. A vast, greater sum of what we do *not* know also grows with time and division of labor. It is useful to plot the track of how "Learners Learn from Standard."

- Call the perfect grasp of cause and effect, **"Reality."** Its track (know-how required to operate perfectly) is not constant: It slopes uphill, away from the learner, as time passes.
- Call the track of a person's accumulation of know-how in time, their learning curve.
- Call current state of group know-how **"Mastery."** Know-how in the form of stored knowledge is not constant: By attrition it slopes downhill away from reality, in time.

Failure to sustain requires no intentional undoing. Not refreshing learning, letting natural attrition and obsolescence run, is all it takes for reality to drift away from best practice.

Learners Learn from Standard

Vast know-how evaporates out of poorly joined exploiting + exploring. Holding adequate mastery hinges on efficient cooperation, to gain lesson-capture out of skirmishes with reality.

Diversity and Variation

March effectively illustrates key factors and interactions in organizational learning. Diversity takes center stage. Sharper than sharp rhetoric, behavior modeling of cause and effect lifts analysis out of political fever swamps.

Standard Learns from Learners

March's central insight: **While learners learn from standard, standard learns from them.** In technocratic compliance cultures standard learns slowly. Reality drags the knowers' establishment kicking, to the lessons of the present. *Generals fight the last war.* The bias is to hire and promote "dream teams" of compliant, fast learners. These are better at chasing mastery than fast-moving reality. Reality marches on with or without us.

In boutiques (like dotcom busts) learners learn lots, fast, on narrow circumstantial advantage. They learn little, slowly, of broader collective wisdom. Reality drags them kicking, to readmit the establishment standards of the past. Shortsighted learners are better at chasing reality than benefiting from mastery. Attrition marches on without us.

This work has big implications for hiring, promotion, compensation, and development:

- **Elites, Fast Learners, Early Adopters**
  - Quickly achieve initial exploitation (return) on stored knowledge
  - Too soon abandon collective wisdom that cost so dearly to accumulate
  - Overspecialize into competency traps and novelty traps
  - **Competence in inferior tactics chokes out superior but not-yet-proficient strategy**
  - Exploit current standard to the detriment of exploration
- **Slow Learners, Conservatives, and Pluggers**
  - Impede exploitation and payback, on the front end
  - Preserve the collective wisdom that cost so dearly to accumulate
  - End up being an anchor for **diversity**, while elites learn fast, resettle sub optimally, early-adopt, prematurely converge
  - Pluggers add to collective wisdom, because **standard learns from their variability** as they struggle to learn from the **standard**

    Slow Learners settle organizational knowledge at a *higher* plane than elites.

    There is great irony in the eventual, greater learning of the slow and "dumb." Normals' systematically higher ceiling, and academic standards getting schooled by accidents, noncompliance, and 'dummies', is mostly lost on elites. Expertise is a fractional thing.
- **Lack of Diversity Truncates the Variability Indispensable to Exploration**
  - Diversity here speaks of behavioral *kata*, not nominal group identification
  - Approach and viewpoint diversity: Manner of acquiring knowledge, skills

- ○ **Dream Teams of elites underperform collaborations of smart and "dumb"**
- ○ **Having some fraction of slow learners is key to organizational learning**
- ○ **Smart–"dumb" collaboration consistently discovers higher eventual knowledge**
- ○ *Amendment, hansei*—where standard learns from the learners— is disproportionately *contributed* by the presence of slow learners. It is disproportionately *realized and exploited into the treasury* by the fast ones. Bill Withers got it so right—*we all need somebody to lean on.*

It has been instructive to consider how learning goes as things run toward equilibrium. But real-life complexity never gets to equilibrate.

External Turbulence and Internal Turnover Impact Sustaining

Evolving causes and effects, competition, and aims continually push reality beyond the current sum of stored knowledge (our standards). Time bends the know-how we need to run well, uphill: It grows away from us as time passes. Fast learning is compliance to the standard of know-how. Note that fast learners evolve toward mastery, which is not reality exactly. As reality mutates, an organization's grasp of it erodes, if there is no turnover of fast learners.

For moderate and fast learners, a little turnover enhances group learning. New orientation introduces diversity, thus, exploration.

Slow learning and turnover are in effect, ways to back into diversity and discovery.

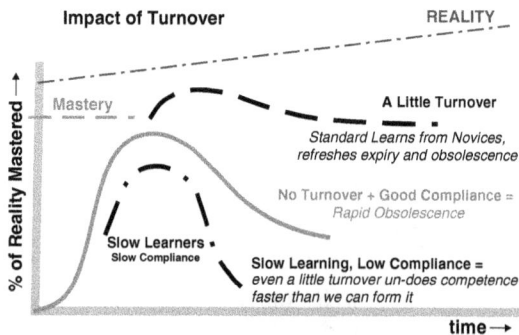

Impact of Turnover   REALITY

% of Reality Mastered →

Mastery

A Little Turnover

Standard Learns from Novices, refreshes expiry and obsolescence

No Turnover + Good Compliance = *Rapid Obsolescence*

Slow Learners • Slow Compliance

Slow Learning, Low Compliance = *even a little turnover un-does competence faster than we can form it*

time →

But in complexity, even light turnover undoes slow learners' struggle to master, faster than fortunate accidents of noncompliance can prop it back up. Organizational learning stands no chance against heavy turnover, or a culture of sloppy compliance, no matter the diversity side effect. Attrition and obsolescence win out.

Tension of "Constancy of Purpose" with Learning Diversity

So far the kind of exploration we have considered was a side effect of noncompliance. Novices and slow learners deviate while they learn, inadvertently exploring. Just because it gets lucky does not mean we should celebrate noncompliance as the corporate ideal. Accidental discovery carries a tradeoff. Noncompliance easily descends into unraveling of control and mutuality.

Turbulence makes it hard to keep up even replacement-rate learning. Our reflex is to double down on *constancy of purpose*: Elites converge on mastery of the establishment view. HR and operations push for zero turnover, grasping at stability. This is understandable.

But micro-retention and micro-compliance wind a double helix of self-defeat, *circling the wagons* around current-state learning. It enshrines current know-how in a way that squeezes the breath out of adaptation. It conflates constancy of purpose with constancy of know-how, effected through the extinction of what brings diversity in learning.

If this reaction stabilizes short-term exploitation, it does so at the expense of exploration. It accelerates the reality gap and decline. There is another, better way to learn in turbulence:

Inoculate for Rapidly Evolving External Reality

Renewal of diversity—background, aims, methods, learning style, tenure—catalyzes learning.

Absent these variations learners learn from standard, but standard stops learning from them. We need diversity, but in a way that doesn't institutionalize antisocial mishaps. The trick is to opportunistically *practice deviation standardly, not accidentally.* Do *active switches* from exploitation to exploration *rather than allowing passive switching to run rampant* and unannounced like guzzlers through a frat house.

The answer is mutual inquiry: Embed coordinated deviation into the standard way of working. The levers we have on this are hiring, training, engineered turnover (cross-flexing), and scheduled recombinance during operations.

What	How
What we shall do is non-negotiable.	*How we may do it is highly negotiable.*
Pursue improvement of normals' ability to comply quicker, in mutuality.	Systematic effort to falsify (improve) standard is routine operations, not a rival add-on if we"have time".
Very intentional compliance distinguishes improvement from just more noise (Shannon's Entropy) when we do PDCA.	Induce tests intentionally, by active switching: Pace-make learning via behavior shifts, not waiting for it to fall from heaven.
Standardize on best we know today, as a platform for adapting tomorrow.	*How* to creatively, jointly test differences is highly negotiable, so long as deliberate.

Michelin Insight

As seen earlier, by training stages Michelin arranges for a diversity of employees to role-swap their domains. A small fraction does the trick. No need to ready human sacrifices for layoff. Intentionality ensures the benefits of turnover and virtuous *"appropriation,"* without resort to *"burning platforms,"* tragedy, and lost training investment. Michelin's holistic practices for *formation* are a corporate poster child.

Honda Insight

Typically, companies design new sites with the aches of old equipment and software in mind. In reaction, they purchase shiny new with bells, whistles, ray guns, and laser beams. Reliability had revolved around wear, age, fatigue, low-tech—tough but predictable. Training, diagnosis, and planning were geared to old-school failure modes.

Digitized, unfamiliar new processes have problems too, only different. They call for new-school paradigms in support. *New wine in old wineskins.* Collective wisdom has not yet been captured into the essence of effective rule-sets for use and upkeep.

This Is Not Your Father's OEE or TPM

Reliability is often so poor on new tech that preventive maintenance gets tabled, to squeeze orders out. This hastens wear and fatigue, and ironically an eventual reprise of the old failure modes. It feeds the decline the new project was meant to counteract.

We just made Frankenstein—a poorly understood bundle of new-age issues, to which we bolt-on the host of old-paradigm problems, through neglect and damage. This is not a tech problem—it is an issue of misjudging what tech launch really encompasses in terms of stored knowledge and the learning *kata* that are called for. Legacy staff endure a long, sharp learning curve. New hires know next-gen, but struggle with legacy equipment kept on in niche service. Commonly, retirees get recalled when old machines and software bring entire sites to heel.

Once we dig a hole, finding capacity to restore a process to norms, and codify new wisdom into a good rule-set, is the gist of **TPM** for these times. Program-driven accounting and training treat the means of production as black boxes: input-output-ROI. Ideas have consequences. We retain no living memory of why it is the way it is, thus how to diagnose and fix. *Lack of diversity begets system fragility.* Many expansions never regain prior levels of **reliability** that once were taken for granted. This is quite serious, across business and industry.

Machines exist to serve and extend people, not the other way around. Wisdom values human support enough to prepare and resource, not just on *how* to use, but *why and how* to upkeep and improve the means itself. Honda recognizes very well the temptations and issues at stake here. When they do an expansion or new site, they go about it very differently:

Opportunity Cost on Human Effort

The system-thinker's paradigm of machines and software is *opportunity cost*. Focus is not on what we are running *from*. It is about what the appliances can help move us *to*: Automation can free doers to extend their span of contribution and control. The meta-agenda is that we go forth and mutually reconnect at our interfaces, to form up novel, added value.

An extended order is not based on shared aims but on mutuality in how we will pursue our several aims. Except in a tribal or individual undertaking, automation won't exist to extend some of the actors' leisure. Nor will it exist to eliminate humans. It serves the extension of value. Automation motivated to replace or amuse ends up socially and economically untenable.

When Honda up-fits a new unit, it does an intentional blend of new and traditional. New sites don't suffer exaggerated proportions of new issues. Old ones don't inordinately suffer dinosaur things. Staff learn to a leveled mix. There is simple strength in Honda's management of reliability, OEE and TPM. Honda expansion is leveling in action.

Marks of a Learning Organization

Executives and HR apply conscious and unconscious category filters in recruiting, placement, reward, and advancement. Ideological filters that truncate diversity of learning *kata* and trying *kata* cast doubt on whether sustainment can even be feasible here.

The aim is to join ourselves with neither all smart, nor all "dumb", nor all old-hands, nor all rookies. Value creation is certainly not consonant with tribalism, *autocracy*, groupthink, or raw individualism. Sustainment shrivels in the ghettos of like-minded knowers, whatever their label. Methodological, ideological, and socio- echo chambers are incubators of decline.

Sustainment thrives where mix is eclectic—anyplace that unlike partners come to feel (act) protectively mutual about compliance to "standard." We may soundly differ, but we join in the conviction that credible disagreement gets tested here, not decreed, not snuck by the group.

Sustainment runs on reassurance that what's right, not who, is going to eventually carry the day. Standard is the best we know today, and we are going to honor it. But just you watch us arrange a try-for-better over the next few days.

CHAPTER 15

Cross-Line Implementation

Most of the knowledge on which we rely . . . is the unintended by-product of others exploring the world in different directions from those we pursue ourselves.[1]

—F.A. Hayek

Stay ready—won't have to get ready.

—Christian Wilkins

A Force Multiplier: "Implicit" Knowledge

Small, cadenced dosing of recombinant trial in routine operation updates group learning toward "reality" not just "mastery." In the best news yet, mishaps are not the only way to get standard to learn from production.

Drug-resistant microbes are live paradigms of adaptation: Their go-to method is genetic crossover. Honda calls it *cross-line implementation*. In continuous processing Box and Draper said "EVOP." By whatever name, it spells next-level breakthrough for efficiency of fitness.

Recombinance

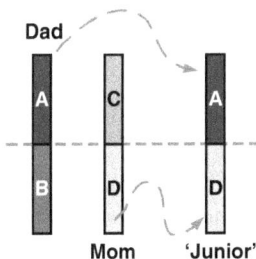

Genetic crossover is recombinance.

It hybridizes success components from the two parents who made it this far.

Part of what makes mom remarkable, is used.

At a crossover, a complement from dad picks up and finishes the recipe.

Jim Manzi begins *Uncontrolled* with a brief, best history of the scientific method.[2] From there he exposits the harnessing of *implicit knowledge* to turbocharge adaptation:

> *"Just guess"* a number between 1 and a billion. Raw trial-and-error can do it, say, if a boss (action, no information) pokes us after each wrong guess. This will take a while. Ouch.
>
> Here is better trial-and-error: information, not just action. Log the wrong guesses. Don't waste any more tries on them. This goes better, but we still get poked—a lot.
>
> Now use *"binary search"*: Instead of "no," Jim informs "high" or "low." First guess (500,000,000) cuts unknown by half. Then by half again—to answer in about 30 guesses.

All the above approaches were trial-and-error. But the *binary* method ran 15 million times faster than brute force. The finest operations produce not just product but information.

> Very roughly speaking, 'just guess' is to binary search as 'introduce random mutations and **retain successes**' is to . . . natural selection.[3]

An ambitious baker could try to improve business by randomly recombining portions, heat, and time. Theoretically, it could be possible for her to blindly knob-twist her way to fame. More likely she will undo the collective wisdom stored in the recipes granny passed on to her for a start, and disappoint the clientele. When something is called "freak of nature" in praise, it is precisely due to the unlikeliness that an accident would turn out so great.

There is a surer way to improve than wagering a bakery's reputation in a recipe lottery. She could have her chemist father visit and regale the clientele with coffee and his experiences with the polymer chemistry of sugars and dough. Dad's cause–effect paradigms can narrow the universe of combinations that the shop might want to try. When they have narrowed down a handful of ideas that seem interesting, brainstorming is pushed to the side. They put on aprons and commence *trystorming*.

They organize an experimental cuisine event and tease palates with novel confections of the hypotheses. They comb the responses for patterns. Feedback focuses their tries further and contributes new lines of inquiry that would not have occurred in the conventional thinking of an old-school chemist. Bakers, chemists, and clientele mutually, iteratively discover novel extensions of value.

PDCA cycling cognitively speeds trial-and-error toward discovery. It sped a Renaissance across Europe, and it can do wonders in a little bakery, too. There is yet another way to boost inquiry to radically greater discovery: recombinance.

> Causal discussions of evolution often imply that mutation is the primary method used to search for new genomes, but in fact **crossover is the workhorse of the search. . . .** Mutations are rare, high-risk bets. Almost all of them fail to improve.[4]

Recombinance in Enterprise

Cross-line implementation intentionally recombines successful segments of discovery from differing domains, into a try.

> it is a system for improvement that develops implicit theories for improvement without the need for conscious intervention . . . it develops and retains implicit knowledge.[5]

Example in Injection Blow Molding

Say a plant molds automotive rack-and-pinion (R&P) boots. Demand spikes. In a fit of exuberance, sales overbooks capacity to the extent that if we stick by plans to shut down for PM and Christmas, we will miss delivery and run The Big Three dry. Bravo for revenue, but this lack of mutuality between sales and production brews a perfect storm of push at their interface.

Technicians want time off for the holidays. Thus motivated, they devise a cooling module to improve R&P cycle time by 9 percent. They can now meet demand, capture market, and still stand on principles (don't skip PMs, and everyone home for holidays). PDCA rescued reliability and mutuality from sacrifice on the altar of *mura* and *muri*.

Great! Why stop here? Let's see where "genetic crossover" might carry this discovery:

> A sister plant makes CVJ boots. Material, tooling, clientele, and specs are different. But . . . recombinance. Splice CVJ's DNA with the segment of R&P's cooling thingamabob. We try this, not because we know, but on principle. Just run the little love-child in a trial. Doing it turns out not exactly plug-and-play: Retrofit onto a CVJ frame makes us offset the trim unit.
>
> The top CVJ reject—*Bad Trim*—drops by 70 percent. Shifting the trimmer mount affected shear angle and blade temperature. We didn't intend it, but at the crossover of cooling, recombined DNA transformed a plain-old trimmer into a freak of nature.

Now, cross back for an additional cycle: Test the altered CVJ shear angle, back into R&P where we began. When we do, it cuts defects by two-thirds in R&P. Crossover in the way we cool autogenerates its own **implicit theories** on shearing and blade temperature—**transcending any need for conscious interventions of masterminds**.

> Wherever possible the rules of the game should be changed to build in this positive bias cumulatively . . . don't just generate trials and retain successes, but that encourage cross pollination and mixing and matching of ideas for improvement.[6]

Cross-Line in Films

Be skeptical of project cheerleaders who claim "same as." Thin and thick films greatly differ in speed, approach angle, web width, stability, and surface. We could cut and paste Tom Rogers' brilliantly simple winding method onto another line. But it had to be reconciled to the new layout, to mount it. Read-across outed hidden conditionals.

Tryout on one line would make us think on our feet, just to coax the new winder arrangement into working at all. Applied on another line, the new rig might come out of the gate even better than the good we did back at the original site of breakthrough.

Splicing one line's spine, with DNA from another's draw or windup, spawned complex creatures that resembled parents, but new traits emerged. Learning enabled us to read discoveries forward, and back to prior installations with new facets of improvement.

Cross-Line in Tires

Once upon a time we industrialized new tire lines from a prototype shop. Scale-up into mass production at Poitiers required adaptation. Other amendments were needed for Ballymena, Spartanburg, Campo Grande, Aranda. The key to making recipe globally manufacturable was intent to falsify—to out hidden conditionals in prototyping. This is an important, cognitive aspect of experiment design.

If we would practice the *gemba* discipline to check-reflect-adjust the launch through a gauntlet of differing means of fabrication, principles sifted back that one could read across oceans for a multiplier effect on cost and performance. Industrialization is no one-way directive of knowledge. Round-robin recombinance discovers far more than modeling, cognitive design, and semi-works proxies.

"Lessons from Labrador"

David Stark recounts how the Naskapi people's ceremonial form of hunting guidance taps recombinance to adaptively sustain through prosperity and challenge. Their shaman

> determined where they would look for game on the next day's hunt by holding a caribou shoulder bone over the fire. Examining the smoke deposits . . . a shaman read for the hunting party the points of . . . tomorrow's search.[7]

Hunting guidance is the product of crossover: One part draws from Brownian Motion of smoke in air. The other part is today's location, and what was found there. A recombinance of the two is joined in the ceremony for tomorrow's plan.

If the Naskapi solely followed meanderings of smoke, each day's plan would be *memoryless*. Success would go on trial-and-error, a novelty trap. It would fail to exploit the already-learned about barren or promising directions to hunt. It would explore at the expense of exploiting stored lessons.

If they purely followed past success, they would perfect their mastery of the known, *which is not the same as mastering reality*. Reality (herds) moves. If we overharvest a rich area, success temporarily rises on depletion of a future. It is a competency trap. Today's success interacts in a complex manner with tomorrow. This is exploiting at the expense of exploration.

Naskapi recombinance does not overplay the linkage of today's success. It does not entirely sever it, either. It works out an adaptive, leveled balance of explore and exploit.

> institutional legacies that retard the quick [static institutionaliza-tion] of immediate successes can be important for keeping open alternative courses of action. **Institutional friction preserves diversity**; it sustains organizational routines that might later be recombined in new organizational forms.[8]

Coaching Fire-and-Forget Out of the Problem-Solving Culture

Here lies a big application for *kata* coaches, A3, and project closers: Often we let solvers imagine they are done, as soon they have stopped the bleeding. Other users are screaming for attention. They did a fine job to get cause on the ground and restrain it. So, we let them go on.

But they didn't kill the issue. We sold their learning out cheaply, for low-hanging fruit. We didn't insist they go on and cut the root. Over time, the loss is gigantic across an enterprise.

Those who don't learn from the past are condemned to repeat it. Juran could confidently coin the *"Pareto"* 80/20 principle because he could be sure of our reliable affair with recurrence. It is a universal feature in problem-solving. Greater even than the self-inflicted pain of recurrence is what we forego when we overlook opportunities to cross-line-implement, for explosive discovery.

Pressured bosses have trouble releasing resources for abstract, delayed gratification like cross-line implementation. We should make it easier to say yes. Devising creative ways to test our hybrids temporarily and *reversibly* is key to making crossover more palatable to the busy. Toward sustainment, we must politely challenge the lazy assumption that an improvement cycle is done when target outcome is achieved. Celebrate, yes. *But an improvement is not "done," until they can answer three questions*:

1. What were the unintended, social consequences of this "solution"?
2. What does this experience suggest should be our next round?
3. Where can we cross-line-implement, to learn what recombinant surprise pops out?

CHAPTER 16

Kasparov's Law

The savage must be able to produce a wide variety of goods and service. . . .

The civilized . . . need know little beyond his accounting or electronics. . . .

Civilization is an enormous device for economizing on knowledge.[1]
—Thomas Sowell

Part 1: Mechanics of How Self-Ordering Systems Work

In complexity there are countless ineffective ways to work. Lean seems to run upstream: It appears to defeat the Second Law of Thermodynamics, by joining partial knowledge and diverging interests into a whole greater than their separate sums. It forms up a system view to efficiently relate our issues of connection. It translates principles and benefits of flow in process industry, into discrete assembly and administration. It adaptively rearranges the connection modes of its actors and appliances, not to homogenize their aims but to re-extend them mutually.

Labor, space utilization, and flowtime routinely improve by half, and defects over 90 percent. ROI is unmatched. Whether in learning, language, markets, or for the level pull of materials, information, and service, this efficient *catallaxy* of coordinating is a revelation.

Part 2: Mechanics of Backsliding

So why do stellar improvements fall to earth or worse? Knowing what to do, being able to, and keeping it up, are all different things. Tribalism is end-connected, instinctual. Pull orders dispersed aims by joining on mutual, abstract rules. Nature is persistent. Smart but counter-instinctive rules, not so much.

Tribal society tries to push its way on how much it knows and conformity of aims. Pull isn't like that: Advancement comes in how *little* we *need* know to excel in our several pursuits.

We have surveyed the great sources on the universals of breakthrough from Juran, Kuhn, Hayek, Hartley, March, Mises, Pareto, Popper, Shannon, Socrates, Sowell, Sproul, and more. Now we will wrap it up with thoughts from Richard Fernandez, Garry Kasparov, and yours truly.

People look to improvement in boom-bust cycles of anomaly-crisis. We instinctually recoil on rules. We would be better served *amending* flaws than to jettison imperfect rules. In mutual learning, we refresh know-how for gentler reformation of aims and efforts.

We considered efficiency: *Takt Attainment* to align, and *stigmergy* to best employ resources in circumstance. Tactics say how best to set ladders up walls. Strategy asks which wall, and why are we climbing, not digging, or going home. It counteracts the drivers of decay. We unpacked triple-loop learning, to adaptively hold proper relation of tactics and strategy.

Part 3: Countermeasures for Breakthrough That Sustains

Lean *exposes*. Exposing is not solving. Leader Standard Work clears the insulation between providers, and users asked to perform upon the standards and support furnished. Given the abstract specialization in value-aiding in a complex enterprise, it is easy for those to get out of line from one another.

Triple-loop learning jailbreaks the within-the-framework learning cycle, to improve the framework itself. It *amends* strategy—capacity, capability, compass heading. Leadership is specialization which balances value-aid in right relation to value-add.

To realize how fractional our knowledge is, is breakthrough in how we start connecting, and to what we don't know. Knowers major on what we know. The learning organization shifts focus onto effectively managing the greater sums of what we *don't* know. Knowers recoil from such admissions. They put *scientistic* faith in inspirational experts. This concentrates power but does little to extend actual order past the short-term.

Complexity's scope can be discouraging, but there is no use in that: When we look up, issues are still there. As history bears out, *catallaxy* offers proven, Renaissance-grade leverage on our issues.

Misplaced Optimism?

We hear much fretting over future subservience to robots and AI over-lords. Hand-wringing recurs in cycles from anomaly to breakthrough. *History rhymes.* Our plight doesn't compare with his—but Erasmus replied to his Age, which was not just figuratively, Dark—*ad fontes.* He and others reasserted a culture of self-assembling improvement. The result was imperfect, but not too shabby.

Tanners maybe thought it the end, when domestically grown fiber-weaving freed neolithic masses from stalking animal skins for loincloths, cloaks, and if lucky some hats and moccasins. Luddites just *knew* it was the end, when water-wheels freed mill hands from actuation of yarn. They could see life was hard and short, with maybe a poor change of clothes and rags for footwear. Then they saw the designers of wheels and gears coming to take them out of their repetitive motion.

Their French cousins wore wooden *sabots* in part because they couldn't afford sewn shoes. S*abotage* was their jamming of *sabots* into the gears, to defy reallocation of human toil. They had trouble seeing the paradigm of **opportunity cost**—the value proposition in what they might do with their efforts once free of the hard monotony of force.

Once water could deliver the rote aspects of brawn, wise ones could re-extend. They thought up what further value they might add, in addition to what the wheel was now doing for them in semiautomatic mode. They could not have pursued these added valuables so long as they remained tied up as brute motive power units.

Invention exploded scarcity and cost. Staples became commonplace. These they rearranged to extend in further unforeseen ways. Life span rose, education, and even leisure, flourished. *Saboteurs* no longer had to suffer wooden shoes.

Opportunity cost: Workers had to forego the task of actuating heavy machinery by muscle power, and its subsistence wage. It turned out to be a nice bargain for all concerned.

"Deep Thinking"

Garry Kasparov's book brings this old story into our robotic present. The chess grandmaster reflects on automation, boiling sustainment down to a paradigm: ***Cognitive Opportunity Cost***.[2] Electronics, materials, sensors . . . artificial intelligence . . . now are rapidly detaching human attendance from non-value-add, or value-aid deemed risky, costly, or burdensome.

Whether this is positive, hangs on how we reapply the minds liberated. Do I join my windfall with others to extend value-add in a novel way? Or spend it on consumption one-and-done (wait for somebody to find me a "next" thing to do, entertainment)? Which I pass up, is the *opportunity cost* of my *knowledge of circumstances of time/place*.

> We haven't lost free will; we have gained time that we don't yet know what to do with. We have gained incredible powers . . . but still lack the sense of purpose to apply them.[3]

Alan Turing made the first chess machine in 1952. Development has pushed on ever since. In 1985 Kasparov became world champion. Like his predecessor, he dispatched his challengers: Until one day in 1997, and then he couldn't. IBM's supercomputer Deep Blue closed the era of unaided human superiority in chess. Turing had in mind a machine that could think like—only better than—us. While Deep Blue impresses Mr. Kasparov, he points out that's not exactly what has transpired.

> Deep Blue was intelligent the way your programmable alarm clock is intelligent. Not that losing to a $10 million alarm clock made me feel any better.[4]

Kasparov took the role of learner from this, not *"gracious loser."* The useful potential of emergent system–human interaction is the real newsflash of cause and effect in complexity.

> Airplanes don't flap their wings and helicopters don't need wings at all. The wheel doesn't exist in nature, but it has served us very well. So why should computer brains work like human brains in order to achieve results?[5]

Kasparov's response to being the representative human who lost to the machines, has been that *Problems Are Treasures.* He spent two decades poking the triple-loop assumptions, considering how people and machines connect. His findings build like this:

1. Grandmasters thrash amateurs.
2. Computers built to excel at the classic approach to chess, thrash grandmasters.

   Computers weigh the fitness of all permutations, and every game in recorded history, faster than master, so no need for truncation or aggregation to ease mental burdens.
3. **Moravec's paradox:** Machines tend to do well where humans are weak and vice versa.

   When arranged so that the strength of one intentionally complements the other's weakness, the combination of [human + machine] emerges formidably. A grandmaster aided by an ordinary PC thrashes the chess-specific supercomputers.

   > Hydra, which was a chess-specific supercomputer like Deep Blue . . . was no match for a strong human player using an ordinary computer. Human strategic guidance combined with the tactical acuity of a computer was overwhelming.[6]
4. In 2005 Playchess ran a sort of cage match, incentivizing "freestyle" arrangements of teamed, solo, grand masters, amateurs, with/without weak or strong computers.

   The winner employed neither supercomputer nor grandmaster. It was a pair of amateurs using three weak PCs. The trick was not the tools, but a *resourceful **method***, their manner of interacting one another and their modest machines:

> Their skill at manipulating and "coaching" their computers to look very deeply into positions effectively counteracted the superior chess understanding of their Grandmaster opponents and the greater computational power of other participants.[7]

5. We come to **Kasparov's Law**[8]—Adaptive method of connection of human–machine effort:

[weak human + machine
+ great process]thrashes   great computer
              or expert
              or (expert + machine + so-so process)

Fujio Cho, of Toyota, put it something like: *We get brilliant results from average people managing brilliant processes. Our competitors get mediocre results from brilliant people managing broken processes.*

The number of possible games that can play out in chess is: 10^{120}

1,000,000,000,000,000,000,000,000,000,000,000,000,

000,000,000,000,000,000,000,000,000,000,000,000,

000,000,000,000,000,000,000,000,000,000,000,000,000

The options of two friends at a checkered toy, pale to the complexity of an enterprise. Still, Richard Fernandez points out, a player just looking eight moves ahead

> is already presented with as many possible games as there are stars in the galaxy. Solving these problems is beyond a machine. It is beyond unaided human capability. But put the two together and. . . .[9]

Toward Sustainment

Process eats outcome-based whack-a-mole schemes. But culture devours process, wherever misalignment forces a choice. Learning organization is cultural embodiment of *Problems Are Treasures*. It leans enterprise forward, using inevitable run-ins with complexity for propulsion.

- Where mutual learning wins out over conformity of knowing as the mode of *interpersonal connection*, it rearranges ambitions into civilized extensions.
- Complementing: [human + tools]
  Tools creatively extend specialization. The acreage a pioneer could order with an axe, a mule, a gun, and a plow could feed a family or more. They left the old country for it.

  Now we do orders of magnitude better with updated tools—tractors, chemicals, and hybrids. In 1900, 98 percent of the United States had to farm. Now 2 percent of the population overfeed the rest, to the point of grain as fuel.
- Division of knowledge [human + tools + adaptive connection method]
  Machines tend to have weaknesses where humans excel (and vice versa).

  Every person has knowledge of circumstance, and stored knowledge that is not up in the "system." Any robot we may gain use of can complement this further. We can shrewdly adapt connection modes among tools and persons in surprising out-workings of gain.

  In recent years, this has been exploited mostly in **customer–supplier** relations. Supply chains have had to learn to meet, not homogenize, dispersed demand. Buyers have forced incredible gains mostly on the back of insisting that suppliers do it. Since the 1980s we have reformed mostly at the ***external*** interfaces, not entirely on mutuality.

What's Next?

The obvious next steps are *physician heal thyself*:

- Cross-line implement these principles for the reform of ***internal*** interfacing.
- Jointly optimize extended value streams to reap inter-enterprise mutuality.

There is much to be gained in learning to reflexively conduct strategy, in *hoshin kanri*. It can bring needed balance to value-aid in the service of value-add. An updated paradigm of strategy would include embedding exploration into routine operation.

With automation, appliances may get updated looks. But the core idea remains the same:

[normals + tools + adaptive connection method] = exploitation that contains efficient, *embedded exploration*. This will produce self-assembling order that learns forward.

"People are capable of doing much, much more than positioning pickles on a patty. They can, with some organization be finding a cure for cancer. . . . Working with smart machines is not so very different as man working with a lathe."[10]

Closing, as We Began

The aim was to lay out system-thinking on how improvement works and the counters that undo it. In reply, we present a behavioral template that can foster the extension of improvement. We have responded on the answering principles of "lean," which can sustain any endeavor that coordinates materials, human effort, time, and treasure in face of variable, alternative uses. That covers a lot of territory, not just factories and distribution centers.

These practices were ordering and extending—nature, language, manufacture, agriculture, trade, exploration—before people could read or write. Don't settle for facile caricatures and mimicking what somebody is said to have done in exotic places. Do system-think in your value-setting. Consider how universal principles of breakthrough and control can translate into your several complexities.

Within chapters, I noted numerous sources for follow-through. Everyone has to start someplace. On the principle of low effort—high impact, a starting reading sequence might be:

Hayek, F.A.—*The Use of Knowledge in Society* (article)
Hayek, F.A.—*The Pretence of Knowledge* (article)

Read, Leonard E.—*I, Pencil* (article)

Rother, Mike—*Toyota Kata*

Juran, J.M.—*Managerial Breakthrough*

Hinken, Brian—*The Learner's Path: Practices for Recovering Knowers*

March, James G.—*Exploration and Exploitation in Organizational Learning* (article)

Taleb, Nassim N.—*Antifragile*

Schwarz, Roger—*The Skilled Facilitator*

Hayek, F.A.—*Law Legislation and Liberty* (Vol. 2)

Where my writing has come up short on style, consider its chapters as trail markers, pointing back at the great sources on learning enterprise. You deserve my best and I have given it.

Now, there you go.

—*Ad Fontes*—

Notes

Introduction and Overview

1. N. N. Taleb. *Antifragile* (New York: Random House, 2012), p. 8.
2. J. K.Liker. *The Toyota Way* (New York: McGraw-Hill, 2004), p. 17.
3. P. Schaff. *The Renaissance: The Revival of Learning and Art in the Fourteenth and Fifteenth Centuries* (New York: G.P. Putnam's Sons, 1891), Particularly Ch. II.
4. *Ibid.*, Ch. XXV–XXVI
5. E. Rummel. "Desiderius Erasmus." *The Stanford Encyclopedia of Philosophy* (Winter 2017 edition), edited by E. N. Zalta. https://plato.stanford.edu/archives/win2017/entries/erasmus

Chapter 1

1. F. A. Hayek. *Law Legislation and Liberty*, Vol. 2 (Chicago: University of Chicago Press, 1976), p. 3.
2. *Ibid.*, p. 35.
3. *Ibid.*, p. 4
4. *Ibid.*, pp. 35–38.
5. *Ibid.*, p. 109.
6. *Ibid.*, p. 111.
7. *Ibid.*, p. 110.
8. *Ibid.*, p. 22.
9. *Ibid.*, p. 23.
10. *Ibid.*, p. 108.
11. *Ibid.*, p. 23.
12. *Ibid.*, p. 3.
13. *Ibid.*, p. 3.
14. F.A. Hayek. "The Use of Knowledge in Society." *The American Economic Review* 35, no. 4, 1945, pp. 519–530. www.jstor.org/stable/1809376
15. S. Camazine, J.-L. 2001. Deneubourg, N. R. Franks, J. Sneyd, G. Theraulaz, and E. Bonabeau. *Self-Organization in Biological Systems* (Princeton: Princeton University Press).
16. D. Sumpter. 2010. *Collective Animal Behavior* (Princeton: Princeton University Press). J. Miller, and S. Page. 2007. *Complex Adaptive Systems*

(Princeton: Princeton University Press). M. Mitchell. 2009. *Complexity: A Guided Tour* (New York: Oxford University Press).

17. F. A. Hayek. *Law Legislation and Liberty*, Vol. 2 (Chicago: University of Chicago Press, 1976), pp. 71, 125

18. P. A. Corning. 1995. "Synergy and Self-Organization in the Evolution of Complex Systems." *Systems Research* 12, pp. 89–121. doi:10.1002/sres.3850120204

19. F. A. Hayek. *Law Legislation and Liberty*, Vol. 2 (Chicago: University of Chicago Press, 1976), Ch. 8.

20. *Ibid.*, p. 38.

21. F. A. Hayek. 1988. *The Fatal Conceit. The Collected Works of F.A. Hayek*, Vol. 1, edited by W.W. Bartley III (Chicago: University of Chicago Press), p. 11.

22. *Ibid.*, p. 12.

23. *Ibid.*, p. 12.

24. *Ibid.*, p. 12.

25. *Ibid.*, p. 41.

26. *Ibid.*, pp. 149–150.

27. *Ibid.*, p. 14.

Chapter 2

1. S. Fleetwood. November 1, 1996. "Order Without Equilibrium: A Critical Realist Interpretation of Hayek's Notion of Spontaneous Order." *Cambridge Journal of Economics* 20, no. 6, pp. 729–747. https://doi-org.libproxy.furman.edu/10.1093/oxfordjournals.cje.a013647

2. F. A. Hayek. 1969 [published 1948]. *Individualism and Economic Order* (Chicago: University of Chicago Press), p. 19.

3. M. Rother. 2010. *Toyota Kata* (New York: McGraw-Hill), p. 15.

4. *Ibid.*, p. 14.

5. *Ibid.*, 2010, p. 19.

6. S. Fleetwood. 2007. *Austrian economics and the analysis of labor markets. The Review of Austrian Economics* 20, p. 247. doi:10.1007/s11138-006-0009-6

7. S. Camazine, J.-L. 2001. Deneubourg, N. R. Franks, J. Sneyd, G. Theraulaz, and E. Bonabeau. *Self-Organization in Biological Systems* (Princeton: Princeton University Press). Ch. 18.

8. *Ibid.*, Chs. 12, 15, 16.

9. D. Reinertsen. 2009. *Product Development Flow* (Redondo Beach, CA: Celeritas), pp. 41, 42, 225.

10. M. Mitchell. 2009. *Complexity: A Guided Tour* (New York: Oxford University Press), pp. 30–39.

11. J. Miller. 2015. *A Crude Look at the Whole* (New York: Basic Books), Ch. 3.

12. R. Adams. April 1, 1996. "The Accident at Chernobyl: What Caused the Explosion?" atomicinsights.com/accident-at-chernobyl-caused-explosion, (accessed February 9, 2018).

13. J. Miller. 2015. *A Crude Look at the Whole* (New York: Basic Books), p, xix.

14. F. A. Hayek. 1979. *The Counter-Revolution of Science: Studies on the Abuse of Reason*, 2nd edition, 1st edition published 1952 (Indianapolis: Liberty Press), p. 70.

Chapter 3

1. A. N. Whitehead. quoted by F. A. Hayek. 1945. "The Use of Knowledge in Society." *The American Economic Review* 35, no. 4, p. 528. www.jstor.org/stable/1809376

2. G. Galsworth. 2011. *Work That Makes Sense* (Portland: Visual-Lean Enterprise Press), pp. 5–6, 36.

3. G. Galsworth. 1997. *Visual Systems* (New York: Amacom), Ch. 2–3.

4. M. Hamel. May 16, 2012. "All I Really Need to Know about Lean I Learned at Waffle House." www.gembatales.com/blog-entry/all-i-really-need-know-about-lean-i-learned-waffle-house-guest-post, (accessed February 7, 2018).

5. S. Camazine, J.-L. 2001. Deneubourg, N. R. Franks, J. Sneyd, G. Theraulaz, and E. Bonabeau. *Self-Organization in Biological Systems* (Princeton: Princeton University Press), pp. 23–26, 56.

6. F. A. Hayek. 1988. *The Fatal Conceit. The Collected Works of F.A. Hayek*, Vol. 1, edited by W.W. Bartley III (Chicago: University of Chicago Press), p. 79.

7. G. P. Box, and N. R. Draper. 1969. *Evolutionary Operation* (New York: John Wiley & Sons), p. 5.

Chapter 4

1. A. Senghas. 21 June 2005. "Language Emergence: Clues from a New Bedouin Sign." *Current Biology* 15, no. 12, pp. R463–R465. search.ebscohost.com/login.aspx?direct=true&db=cmedm&AN=15964267&site=ehost-live, (accessed February 7, 2018).

2. J. J. Hublin, A. Ben-Ncer, S. E., Bailey, S. E., Freidline, S., Neubauer, M. M., Skinner, I., Bergmann, A., Le Cabec, S., Benazzi, K., Harvati, and P. Gunz. June 7, 2017. "New Fossils from Jebel Irhoud, Morocco and the Pan-African Origin of Homo Sapiens." *Nature* 546, no. 7657, pp. 289–292.

EBSCOhost, doi:10.1038/nature22336. *See also,* E. Yong. June 7, 2017. "Scientists Have Found the Oldest Known Human Fossils." https://www .theatlantic.com/science/archive/2017/06/the-oldest-known-human-fos-sils-have-been-found-in-an-unusual-place/529452

3. S. Camazine, J.-L. 2001. Deneubourg, N. R. Franks, J. Sneyd, G. Theraulaz, and E. Bonabeau. *Self-Organization in Biological Systems* (Princeton: Princeton University Press), p. 31.

4. *Ibid.,* Ch. 2.

5. *Ibid.,* p. 24.

6. *Ibid.,* pp. 22–23.

7. J. M. Juran. 1989. *Quality Improvement Tools: Data Collection,* Fifth Print-ing, (Wilton, CT: Juran Institute), p. 1.

8. S. Camazine, J.-L. 2001. Deneubourg, N. R. Franks, J. Sneyd, G. Theraulaz, and E. Bonabeau. *Self-Organization in Biological Systems* (Princeton: Princeton University Press), Ch. 4.

9. *Ibid.,* p. 48.

10. *Ibid.,* p. 49.

11. H. Ford. 1988 [originally published 1926]. *Today and Tomorrow,* Special Edition of Ford's 1926 Classic. (Portland: Productivity Press), p. 82.

12. W. Hopp, and M. Spearman. 2001. *Factory Physics,* 2nd edition (Boston: Irwin McGraw-Hill), pp. 339–363.

13. S. Camazine, J.-L. 2001. Deneubourg, N. R. Franks, J. Sneyd, G. Theraulaz, and E. Bonabeau. *Self-Organization in Biological Systems* (Princeton: Princeton University Press), pp. 23–26.

14. D. Stark. n.d. "Heterarchy: Asset Ambiguity, Organizational Innovation, and the Postsocialist Firm." (CAHRS Working Paper #96–21). Ithaca, NY: Cornell University, School of Industrial and Labor Relations, Center for Advanced Human Resources Studies. http://digitalcommons.ilr.cor-nell.edu/cahrswp/190. Especially p. 28. Hayek. 1973. *The Fatal Conceit* (London: Relating the work of Moses Finley on heterarchy, An Ancient Economy), p. 12. J. F. Padgett. November 1992. "Learning from (and about) March." *Contemporary Sociology* 21, no. 6, pp. 744–749. search. ebscohost.com/login.aspx?direct=true&db=fmh&AN=9301102861&sit e=ehost-live. (accessed February 7, 2018). D. Wengrow and D. Graeber. September 2015. "Farewell to the 'Childhood of Man': Ritual, Seasonality, and the Origins of Inequality." *Journal of the Royal Anthropological Institute* 21, no. 3, pp. 597–619. EBSCOhost, doi:10.1111/1467-9655.12247. C. L. Crumley. 1995. "Heterarchy and the Analysis of Complex Societies." *Archeological Papers of the American Anthropological Association* 6, pp. 1–5.

doi:10.1525/ap3a.1995.6.1.1. E. Graham. March 2005. "Maya Political History" [Review article]. *Antiquity* 79, pp. 210–214. EBSCOhost, search. ebscohost.com/login.aspx?direct=true&db=brd&AN=505112951&site =ehost-live

15.   D. Reinertsen. 2009. *Product Development Flow* (Redondo Beach, CA: Celeritas), pp. 251–266.

16.   P. Corning. 1995. "Synergy and Self-Organization in the Evolution of Complex Systems." *Systems Research* 12, pp. 89–121. doi:10.1002/ sres.3850120204

17.   *Ibid.*, p. 106.

18.   A. B. Sendova-Franks and N. R. Franks. 1999. "Self-Assembly, Self-Organization and Division of Labour." *Philosophical Transactions: Biological Sciences* 354, no. 1388, pp. 1395–1405. www.jstor.org/ stable/57032

Chapter 5

1.   J. M. Juran. 1964. *Managerial Breakthrough* (New York: McGraw-Hill), p. 3.

2.   T. S. Kuhn. 2012 [Originally published 1962]. *The Structure of Scientific Revolutions*, 4th edition. (Chicago: University of Chicago Press), p. 2.

3.   J. M.Juran, *Managerial Breakthrough*, p. 3.

4.   *Ibid.*, p. 24.

5.   *Ibid.*, p. 38.

6.   I. Hacking. 2012. "Introductory Essay to Kuhn." T. S. Kuhn. 2012 [Originally published 1962]. *The Structure of Scientific Revolutions*, 4th edition. (Chicago: University of Chicago Press), p. xxvii.

7.   T. S. Kuhn. *The Structure of Scientific Revolutions*, p. 149.

8.   *Ibid.*, Ch. XII

9.   J. M. Juran. 1989. *Quality Improvement Tools: Problem Solving/Glossary*, Fifth Printing (Wilton, CT: Juran Institute), p. 1.

10.   J. M. Juran. 1944. *Bureaucracy* (New York: Harper & Brothers), pp. ix–xii.

11.   L. Mises. 1944. *Bureaucracy* (New Haven, CT: Yale University Press). EB-SCOhost, search.ebscohost.com/login.aspx?direct=true&db=brr&AN=6 7933127&site=ehost-live. p. 47, (accessed February 7, 2018).

12.   J. M. Juran. *Quality Improvement Tools: Problem Solving Glossary*, pp. 14–21.

13.   J. M. Juran. *Managerial Breakthrough*, pp. 141–142.

Chapter 7

1. F.A. Hayek. "The Use of Knowledge in Society." *The American Economic Review* 35, no. 4, 1945, p. 519. www.jstor.org/stable/1809376

Chapter 8

1. J. M. Juran. 1944. *Bureaucracy* (New York: Harper & Brothers), p. 1.
2. *Ibid.*, p. 41.
3. J. M. Juran. 1964. *Managerial Breakthrough* (New York: McGraw-Hill), pp. 29–41.
4. G. Galsworth. 1997. *Visual Systems* (New York: Amacom), p. 181.
5. J. M. Juran. July 1955. "Dealing With the 'Obstructionist' Superintendent." *Industrial Quality Control* 12, no. 1. Reprint with permission of American Society for Quality, November 20, 2017.

Chapter 9

1. "Clarke's Laws." October 2017. *Computer Desktop Encyclopedia*, p. 1. EBSCOhost, search.ebscohost.com/login.aspx?direct=true&db=sch&AN=125635533&site=ehost-live
2. R. Fernandez. December 14, 2016. "James T. Putin." https://pjmedia.com/richardfernandez/2016/12/14/james-t-putin/2
3. F. W. Taylor. 1914. *The Principles of Scientific Management* (New York: Harper & Brothers), p. 83.
4. K. R. Popper. 1968. *The Logic of Scientific Discovery* (New York: Routledge), first published 1934. p. xix.
5. K. R. Popper. 1963. *Conjectures and Refutations: The Growth of Scientific Knowledge* (New York: Basic books). EBSCOhost, search.ebscohost.com/login.aspx?direct=true&db=brr&AN=68006914&site=ehost-live, Ch. 1.
6. F. A. Hayek. 1979. *The Counter-Revolution of Science: Studies on the Abuse of Reason*, 2 edition, 1st edition published 1952 (Indianapolis: Liberty Press), p. 114.
7. *Ibid.*, p. 80.
8. *Ibid.*, p. 87.

Chapter 10

1. P. A. Corning. 1995. "Synergy and Self-Organization in the Evolution of Complex Systems." *Systems Research* 12, pp. 89–121. doi:10.1002/sres.3850120204

2. R. C. Sproul. 2000. *The Consequences of Ideas* (Wheaton, IL: Crossway), p. 47.

3. J. Miller. 2015. *A Crude Look at the Whole* (New York: Basic Books), pp. 2–5, 9, 12, 22, 62, 228. *also see* M. Mitchell. 2009. *Complexity: A Guided Tour* (New York: Oxford University Press), pp. ix–x.

4. P. A. Corning. 1995. "Synergy and Self-Organization in the Evolution of Complex Systems." *Systems Research* 12, pp. 89–121. doi:10.1002/sres.3850120204

5. *Ibid.*

6. E. Mayr, cited by P. Corning. 1995. *Synergy and self-organization in the evolution of complex systems.*

7. R. Schwarz. 2017. *The Skilled Facilitator* (Hoboken, NJ: Jossey-Bass), pp. 103–116. Originally copyrighted 1994.

8. F. A. Hayek. 2014. "Friedrich August von Hayek—Prize Lecture: The Pretence of Knowledge." http://www.nobelprize.org/nobel_prizes/economic-sciences/laureates/1974/hayek-lecture.html, (accessed February 10, 2018).

9. F. A. Hayek. 2001 [Originally published 1960]. *The Constitution of Liberty.* The Definitive Edition. The Collected Works of F.A. Hayek, vol. XVII, edited by W.W. Bartley III (Chicago: University of Chicago Press), p. 130.

10. T. S. Kuhn. 2012 [Originally published 1962]. *The Structure of Scientific Revolutions*, 4th edition. (Chicago: University of Chicago Press), p. 75.

Chapter 11

1. F. A. Hayek. 1969 [published 1948]. *Individualism and Economic Order* (Chicago: University of Chicago Press), p. 19.

2. R. Schwarz. 2017. *The Skilled Facilitator* (Hoboken, NJ: Jossey-Bass), p. 92. Originally copyrighted 1994.

3. F. A. Hayek. "The Use of Knowledge in Society." *The American Economic Review* 35, no. 4, 1945, pp. 521–522. www.jstor.org/stable/1809376

4. *Ibid.*, p. 524.

5. *Ibid.*, p. 526.

6. *Ibid.*, p. 526.

7. *Ibid.*, p. 527.

8. *Ibid.*, p. 530.

9. *Ibid.*, p. 527.

10. *Ibid.*, p. 530.

11. T. S. Kuhn. 2012 [Originally published 1962]. *The Structure of Scientific Revolutions*, 4th edition. (Chicago: University of Chicago Press), p. 156.

Chapter 12

1. Socrates, quoted by Popper, K.R. 1957 [Originally published 1945]. *The Open Society and Its Enemies, Vol 1, The Spell of Plato*, 3rd Edition. (London: Routledge & Kegan Paul Ltd), p. 130.

2. F. A. Hayek. 1969 [published 1948]. *Individualism and Economic Order* (Chicago: University of Chicago Press), p. 19.

3. D. Stark. January–March 2001. "Heterarchy: Exploiting Ambiguity and Organizing Diversity." *Brazilian Journal of Political Economy* 21, no. 1, p. 81. http://www.rep.org.br/pdf/81-2.pdf, (accessed February 7, 2018).

4. B. Hinken. 2007. *The Learner's Path: Practices for Recovering Knowers* (Wortham, MA: Pegasus Communications, Inc.).

5. C. Argyris. 2015. *Double-Loop Learning*, vol. 11 (Wiley Encyclopedia of Management), pp. 1–2.

6. J. K. Liker. 2004. *The Toyota Way* (New York: McGraw-Hill), Ch. 20.

7. F. W. Taylor. 1914. *The Principles of Scientific Management* (New York: Harper & Brothers), p. 83.

8. A. Senghas. 21 June 2005. "Language Emergence: Clues from a New Bedouin Sign." *Current Biology* 15, no. 12, pp. R463–R465. search.ebscohost.com/login.aspx?direct=true&db=cmedm&AN=15964267&site=ehost-live, (accessed February 7, 2018).

9. J. M. Juran. 1989. *Quality Improvement Tools: Data Collection*, Fifth Printing, (Wilton, CT: Juran Institute), pp. 1–3.

10. R. C. Sproul. 2000. *The Consequences of Ideas* (Wheaton, IL: Crossway), p. 27.

11. Socrates, quoted by Popper, K.R. 1957 [Originally published 1945]. *The Open Society and Its Enemies, Vol 1, The Spell of Plato*, 3rd Edition. (London: Routledge & Kegan Paul Ltd), p. 130.

Chapter 13

1. L. A. White. 1948. "Man's Control over Civilization: An Anthropocentric Illusion." *The Scientific Monthly* 66, no. 3, pp. 235–247. www.jstor.org/stable/19284

2. M. Rother. 2018. "Improvement Kata—A Scientific Pattern to Practice." www-personal.umich.edu/~mrother/KATA_Files/IK_Reference_Guide.pdf, (accessed February 7, 2018).

3. L. E. Read. 1999. "I, Pencil: My Family Tree as Told to Leonard E. Read." *Library of Economics and Liberty*. http://www.econlib.org/library/Essays/rdPncl1.html, (accessed February 7, 2018).

4. V. Pareto, cited by F. A. v. Hayek. 1940. "Socialist Calculation: The Competitive 'Solution'." *Economica* 7, no. 26, p. 126. www.jstor.org/stable/2548692

5. F. A. v. Hayek. 1940. "Socialist Calculation: The Competitive 'Solution'." *Economica* 7, no. 26, p. 126. www.jstor.org/stable/2548692.

6. F. A. Hayek. 2001 [Originally published 1960]. *The Constitution of Liberty.* The Definitive Edition. The Collected Works of F. A. Hayek, vol. XVII, edited by W.W. Bartley III (Chicago: University of Chicago Press), p. 75.

7. *Ibid.*, Ch. 2.

8. *Ibid.*, p. 73.

9. *Ibid.*, p. 75.

10. *Ibid.*, p. 75.

11. *Ibid.*, p. 80.

12. W. A. Lewis. 1955. *The Theory of Economic Growth* (London: Routledge), p. 172.

13. B. E. Kline and N. H. Martin. May/June 1958 "Freedom, Authority, and Decentralization." *Harvard Business Review* 36, no. 3, p. 70. EBSCOhost, search.ebscohost.com/login.aspx?direct=true&db=bth&AN=6779177& site=ehost-live, (accessed February 7, 2018).

Chapter 14

1. S. Kates. 2014. *Free Market Economics.* 2nd edition (Cheltenham: Edward Elgar), Ch. 3.

2. F. Bastiat. 1995. "What Is Seen and What Is Not Seen." Selected Essays on Political Economy. Seymour Cain, trans. *Library of Economics and Liberty*, February 10, 2018. http://www.econlib.org/library/Bastiat/basEss1.html, (accessed February 7, 2018).

3. S. Covey. 2004 [Originally published 1989]. *The Seven Habits of Highly Successful People* (New York: Free Press), p. 54.

4. J. G. March. February 1991. "Exploration and Exploitation in Organizational Learning." *Organization Science* 2, no. 1, pp. 71–87. EBSCOhost, search.ebscohost.com/login.aspx?direct=true&db=bth&AN=4433770& site=ehost-live, (accessed February 7, 2018).

Chapter 15

1. F. A. Hayek. *Law Legislation and Liberty*, Vol. 2 (Chicago: University of Chicago Press, 1976), p. 111.

2. J. Manzi. 2012. *Uncontrolled: The Surprising Payoff of Trial-and-Error for Business, Politics, and Society* (New York: Basic Books), Chs. 1–3.

3. *Ibid.*, p. 32.
4. *Ibid.*, p. 36.
5. *Ibid.*, p. 33.
6. *Ibid.*, p. 37.
7. S. Stark. 1996. "Heterarchy: Asset ambiguity, organizational innovation, and the Postsocialist Firm". *CAHRS Working Paper #96–21*. Ithaca, NY: Cornell University, School of Industrial and Labor Relations, Center for Advanced Human Resource Studies. http://digitalcommons.ilr.cornell.edu/cahrswp/190, (accessed February 7, 2018).
8. *Ibid.*, p. 5

Chapter 16

1. T. Sowell. 1980. *Knowledge & Decisions* (New York: Basic Books), p. 7.
2. G. Kasparov. 2017. *Deep Thinking* (New York: Public Affairs), pp. 225–226.
3. *Ibid.*, p. 225.
4. *Ibid.*, 2017. p. 4.
5. *Ibid.*, p. 27.
6. *Ibid.*, p. 246.
7. *Ibid.*, p. 246.
8. *Ibid.*, p. 247.
9. R. Fernandez. January 15, 2014. "The Fearful Future." https://pjmedia.com/richardfernandez/2014/1/15/the-fearful-future
10. *Ibid.*

About the Author

W. Scott Culberson is a system-thinker, an architect of P&L achievement through lean transformation and learning organization. He brings experience from process–product development, design of production systems, control, logistics, quality-intensive plant management, corporate technical apprenticeship, multinational startup, turn-around, and consultancy in operational excellence.

He has delivered high-ROI results in continuous processing, discrete assembly, planning, logistic, retail, service-repair, admin, transactional, manufacturability, and reliability. Scope includes automotive, power tools, appliances, capital equipment, mining, refining, construction and engineering materials, publication and broadcast, architecture, food, pharma, electronics, metal forming, polymerization, fiber, films, and packaging printing and conversion.

Scott is a chemical engineering graduate of Clemson University. He speaks fluent French and basic German, from expatriations in Europe.

Index

OTHER TITLES IN OUR SUPPLY AND OPERATIONS MANAGEMENT COLLECTION

Joy M. Field, Boston College, *Editor*

- *Contemporary Issues in Supply Chain Management and Logistics* by Anthony M.Pagano and Mellissa Gyimah
- *Understanding the Complexity of Emergency Supply Chains* by Matt Shatzkin
- *Mastering Leadership Alignment: Linking Value Creation to Cash Flow* by Jahn Ballard and Andrew Bargerstock
- *Statistical Process Control for Managers, Second Edition* by Victor Sower
- *Sustainable Operations and Closed Loop Supply Chains, Second Edition* by Gilvan Souza
- *The High Cost of Low Prices: A Roadmap to Sustainable Prosperity* by David S. Jacoby
- *The Global Supply Chain and Risk Management* by Stuart Rosenberg
- *Insightful Quality, Second Edition: Beyond Continuous Improvement* by Victor E. Sower
- *Managing Using the Diamond Principle: Innovating to Effect Organizational Process Improvement* by Mark W. Johnson

Announcing the Business Expert Press Digital Library

Concise e-books business students need for classroom and research

This book can also be purchased in an e-book collection by your library as

- a one-time purchase,
- that is owned forever,
- allows for simultaneous readers,
- has no restrictions on printing, and
- can be downloaded as PDFs from within the library community.

Our digital library collections are a great solution to beat the rising cost of textbooks. E-books can be loaded into their course management systems or onto students' e-book readers.

The **Business Expert Press** digital libraries are very affordable, with no obligation to buy in future years. For more information, please visit **www.businessexpertpress.com/librarians**. To set up a trial in the United States, please email **sales@businessexpertpress.com**.

.

www.ingramcontent.com/pod-product-compliance
Lightning Source LLC
Chambersburg PA
CBHW070459200326
41519CB00013B/2647